I0559913

Deeper Minds

Navigate Your Mind, Overcome Barriers, and

Achieve Lasting Success

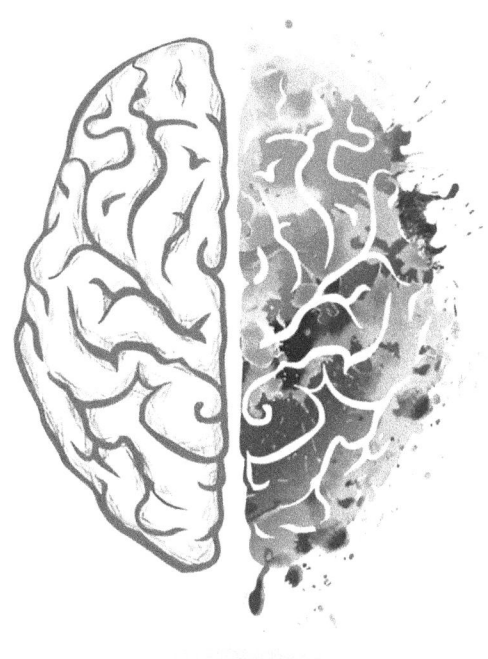

Lynnette A. Bauer

Published by Book Writing Pioneer

Cover design by Book Writing Pioneer

ISBN: Printed in the United States

TABLE OF CONTENTS

CHAPTER 1

NEW BEGINNINGS AND TAKING RISKS

The Uncharted Path

Life is a journey of constant evolution—a series of beginnings, transitions, and endings that shape who we are and who we are becoming. Every moment presents an opportunity to step into something new, to venture down an unmarked path filled with both challenges and discoveries. The energy of new beginnings is both exciting and intimidating. It holds the promise of growth, the opening of new doors, and the courage to step into the unknown.

There's a magical moment just before anything begins—before a new relationship, a career change, a creative project, or a personal transformation. It's the void, a space that is empty yet brimming with infinite possibility. In this space, the energy of spontaneity thrives. You stand at the edge of something unknown, heart racing with anticipation.

1

The future is unwritten, and all paths are open. This is where the spark of creation lives and where the most profound transformations take shape. But to step into this energy, you must summon courage—the courage to let go of control, take risks, and trust that the journey will unfold as it is meant to.

Every new beginning is an adventure. It's a step into uncharted territory where you may not know exactly where you'll end up—and that's the beauty of it. Life doesn't follow a straight line; it ebbs and flows, filled with detours and unexpected turns. It's in these unplanned moments— when we take risks and let go of our fears—that we often find our truest selves and the greatest rewards. These moments shape us, not because they are easy, but because they challenge us to grow in ways we never expected.

The Energy of Spontaneity and Risk

Spontaneity is the lifeblood of creativity, adventure, and joy. It's the ability to act without overthinking—to trust the moment and let things unfold naturally. Spontaneous action often takes us out of our comfort zone, requiring us to relinquish control and trust in the flow of life. While this can be unsettling, it is also where the magic happens.

When we embrace spontaneity, we tap into an energy that allows us to make bold choices, take risks, and experience life more fully. Spontaneity invites us to break free from rigid plans and expectations. It's the force that pushes us to say yes when fear urges us to say no—and often, these are the moments when we feel most alive. The more we learn to listen to our impulses, to the voice of curiosity and adventure within us, the more we allow life to unfold with joy and creativity.

Taking risks is essential to living fully. It is through risk-taking that we break free from the limitations we impose upon ourselves, discovering new strengths and capabilities along the way. A risk might be something as small as trying a new hobby or reaching out to someone we admire, or as big as moving to a new city, starting a business, or embarking on a personal transformation. Each risk carries the potential for growth and self-discovery, and it often teaches us the most profound lessons.

The Void Before Creation: A Space of Infinite Potential

Before creation can happen, there is always a period of stillness, emptiness, and potential—a fresh start, an open heart, and a willingness to leap into the unknown. As we stand at the beginning, we are unaware of what lies ahead but trust that the journey will unfold exactly as it's meant to. Life is full of boundless potential, and every new beginning requires the courage to take that first step.

In life, we often stand at a metaphorical cliff, looking out at the unknown. We may feel the pull of new possibilities, but also the fear of what might go wrong. The void before creation is a place where we must surrender to the flow of life and trust that we will be guided. It is here that our dreams are born. In this emptiness, we have the space to create our own path, free from the constraints of old patterns and limitations.

Every new opportunity, whether big or small, exists in this space of potential. When we step into it with an open heart, we allow ourselves to be shaped by the process of creation itself. The act of creation isn't just about producing something tangible—it's about opening ourselves up to the unfolding journey of life, where the destination is as much about the growth we experience along the way as it is about the end result.

Embracing Fear of Failure: Shedding Old Limitations

The fear of failure is one of the greatest barriers to stepping into the energy of new beginnings. It whispers in our ears, convincing us that we're not ready, that we're not enough, that we don't deserve success. This voice comes from past experiences, from old stories we tell ourselves, and from societal pressures that define success in narrow ways.

But the truth is, failure is part of the process. Every successful person, every great innovation, and every meaningful relationship has been built on the foundation of trying, failing, learning, and trying again. Failure is not an end—it is a lesson, an opportunity for growth, and a stepping stone toward greater success. When we release our attachment to the idea of perfection, we free ourselves to embrace the unknown with confidence and grace.

Instead of fearing failure, we must learn to embrace it as part of the creative process. With each risk we take, we come closer to uncovering who we truly are. And when we step into the unknown without fear, we find that the universe has a way of supporting us in ways we couldn't have imagined. The journey itself becomes the reward.

Life Lesson: Embracing New Opportunities with an Open Heart

The life lesson is simple yet powerful: embrace new opportunities with an open heart. Life is constantly presenting us with chances for growth, adventure, and self-discovery. But to fully embrace these opportunities, we must approach them with openness, curiosity, and a willingness to step into the unknown.

Whether it's embarking on a new career, meeting new people, or exploring new ways of thinking, every new opportunity invites us to discover something new about ourselves. These experiences are the catalysts for our personal evolution. By seeing each new path as a chance to grow, learn, and expand, we allow ourselves to be transformed by the very act of stepping into the unknown.

The journey may be filled with unexpected turns, and the path may not always be clear. But if we embrace it with courage and curiosity, we will find that each step brings us closer to understanding our true potential. Life's greatest adventures begin when we say "yes" to the unknown, shedding our fear of failure and trusting that we are exactly where we need to be.

Practical Exercise: Stepping Into the Unknown

To help you embrace the energy of new beginnings, try this exercise:

1. Identify an Area of Fear – Think of an area in your life where you feel fear or resistance to taking a step forward. It could be a new job, a creative project, a relationship, or even a small habit you've been wanting to change.

2. Challenge Your Fear – Write down what specifically scares you about taking this step. Be honest with yourself about your fears and doubts. Then ask yourself: What could I gain by embracing this opportunity? What new experiences or lessons are waiting for me?

3. Identify one small, actionable step you can take toward this new beginning. It might be making a phone call, doing research, or setting a goal for the week. The key is to take action—no matter how small—and move forward.

4. Embrace the Process – As you take this step, focus on the journey rather than the outcome. Trust that each move you make is a chance to grow, even if the path isn't always clear. Celebrate your willingness to try something new.

5. Reflect and Celebrate – After taking that step, reflect on how it felt. What did you learn? Celebrate the courage it took to move forward, and recognize that every step you take is a victory.

By embracing new beginnings, spontaneity, and the courage to take risks, we unlock life's boundless potential. The energy of creation is always present, waiting for us to access it. When we shed our fears and step into the unknown with curiosity and confidence, we set ourselves on a path of growth, joy, and self-discovery.

CHAPTER 2

HARNESSING PERSONAL POWER

Unlocking Your Inner Strength

In the journey of life, there comes a pivotal moment when you realize that the power to create change, transform your reality, and shape your future lies within you. This realization is the essence of personal power—the ability to tap into your inner strengths, talents, and confidence and channel them toward achieving your desires. Harnessing personal power means becoming the conscious architect of your life, making empowered decisions, and taking ownership of your actions.

Too often, we are led to believe that external circumstances dictate our success, happiness, and fulfillment. However, true personal power is about taking full responsibility for our lives recognizing that our thoughts, beliefs, and actions shape the reality we experience. Life is not something that merely happens to us; it is something we actively participate in and mold with every choice we make. The power to manifest, lead, and create lies within our hands, waiting to be awakened.

Mastery of Self: Confidence and Conscious Creation

At the core of personal power is self-mastery—the ability to understand and direct your own thoughts, emotions, and behaviors with purpose. When we master ourselves, we gain the ability to respond to life's challenges with clarity, calm, and focus rather than reacting out of fear, doubt, or frustration. Personal mastery requires both awareness and discipline. It's about understanding your inner world and learning how to steer it toward your goals.

This mastery is rooted in confidence—a belief in your ability to succeed and navigate challenges. Confidence is not an innate trait reserved for a select few; it is a muscle that can be developed over time with practice and intentionality. It grows when we make decisions based on our true values, act with integrity, and take risks. Confidence flourishes when we stop seeking external validation and instead trust in our own judgment and abilities.

Once we develop confidence in ourselves, we begin to create the life we desire consciously. Manifestation is the process of turning our intentions into reality. By clarifying our desires, aligning our thoughts and actions with our goals, and releasing doubts and fears, we attract the right opportunities, resources, and people into our lives. Personal power isn't just about taking action—it's about cultivating a mindset of abundance and possibility. When we believe in our power to create, the universe responds in kind.

Leadership and Individuality: Owning Your Journey

Harnessing your personal power also involves stepping into the role of a leader in your own life. This doesn't mean leading others in a traditional sense but rather taking charge of your own path with confidence and vision. Leadership is about making decisions that align with your higher self, setting clear intentions, and taking the initiative to move forward—even when the path is unclear.

Leadership also means embracing individuality—being true to who you are and owning your unique gifts and talents. The world doesn't need more copies of others; it needs the real you. It's easy to fall into the trap of comparison, but true power comes from embracing your individuality and recognizing that your perspective and talents are your greatest assets. You are not here to follow in anyone else's footsteps—you are here to blaze your own trail with courage, authenticity, and conviction.

Embodying your individuality means letting go of the fear of judgment, rejection, or failure. It means being unapologetically yourself and trusting that your contributions are valuable. By doing so, you empower others to do the same, creating a ripple effect of personal empowerment in the world around you.

Taking the initiative: The First Step Toward Change

To truly harness your personal power, you must take the initiative— the willingness to move beyond mere intention and actively step into action. Change does not happen by waiting for the perfect moment or ideal circumstances; it happens when we decide to act, even in the face of uncertainty.

Taking initiative means being proactive instead of reactive. It's about making decisions with purpose rather than allowing external forces to dictate your direction. Every time you take a step toward your goals, you signal to yourself and the universe that you are in charge of your life. Each step forward builds momentum, turning dreams into tangible outcomes.

Remember, taking initiative doesn't always mean making giant leaps. Often, it's about starting small—setting clear goals, breaking them down into manageable actions, and making consistent progress. When you take these small steps with confidence, they lead to bigger opportunities and greater success.

Life Lesson: Empower Yourself to Manifest Your Goals with Clarity and Purpose

The key takeaway here is to empower yourself to manifest your goals with clarity, confidence, and purpose. To do this, you must first believe in your ability to create the life you desire. Personal power is not just about action; it's about aligning your thoughts, emotions, and energy with your intentions. When you are clear about what you want and take purposeful steps toward it, you attract the right opportunities and resources into your life.

Guiding Principles to Harness Your Personal Power:

1. Clarity of Vision – The first step toward manifesting your goals is defining what you truly want. Spend time reflecting on your desires, dreams, and values. Write them down and create a vision for your life. The clearer you are, the easier it becomes to align your actions with your goals.

2. Belief in Yourself – Confidence is the foundation of personal power. Trust that you have everything you need to create the life you want. Even in the face of obstacles or setbacks, remember that your power to overcome them comes from within.

3. Consistent Action – Manifestation requires effort. Take small steps every day toward your goals. Whether it's making a phone call, doing research, or building new habits, every action moves you closer to your desired outcome.

4. Trust the Process – Have faith that the universe will provide what you need at the right time. Trust in the timing of your journey, knowing that everything unfolds for your highest good, even if it doesn't initially appear as expected.

5. Self-Reflection and Growth – As you progress, take time to reflect on your journey. Celebrate successes, learn from failures, and continuously refine your vision. Personal growth is a journey, not a destination, and it is through this process that you truly harness your power.

Practical Exercise: Harnessing Your Personal Power

To begin tapping into your personal power, try this simple yet powerful exercise:

1. Identify Your Strengths – Write down a list of your strengths and skills. What are you naturally good at? What unique talents set you apart? Reflect on moments when you felt truly empowered and confident—what qualities were present?

2. Set Clear Intentions – Choose one goal or desire you want to manifest. Be specific: What do you want to achieve, and by when? Write down your intention in measurable terms.

3. Break It Down – Divide your goal into smaller, actionable steps. What are three things you can do right now to move toward your goal? Commit to taking one action each day.

4. Visualize Your Success – Close your eyes and imagine yourself having already achieved your goal. What does it feel like? What does your life look like? Hold this vision in your mind and let it fuel your actions.

5. Take the First Step – Commit to taking at least one step toward your goal today. It doesn't need to be perfect, but it must be intentional. Every small action builds momentum.

Mastering Your Life with Intention

In life's journey, personal power is your greatest asset. It is the force that allows you to break free from limitations, seize opportunities, and create a life that aligns with your highest self. By embracing confidence, trusting in your ability to manifest, and taking bold actions with clarity and purpose, you tap into the unlimited potential within you.

Personal power is not about controlling others—it is about mastering your own life and creating the world you desire, one intentional step at a time.

CHAPTER 3

LISTENING TO YOUR INTUITION

Navigating the Inner Realm

In the unfolding journey of life, we often find ourselves at crossroads—moments where logic alone cannot provide the answers, and the path ahead feels unclear. It is in these moments that intuition, that quiet inner voice, becomes our most trusted guide. Intuition is not just a mystical concept or abstract wisdom; it is a deep, inherent knowing that we all carry within us. Learning to trust this inner wisdom and embracing the balance between logic and intuition can transform the way we move through the world.

The journey toward deep listening involves recognizing and honing this powerful, often underused sense. Intuition is like an inner compass, a tool that helps us navigate the mysteries of life, particularly in moments of confusion, uncertainty, or spiritual growth. While logic gives us structure, intuition opens the door to a greater, often unseen realm of wisdom. By learning to cultivate and trust our intuition, we connect with a source of knowledge that transcends the limitations of the rational mind.

The Mystery of Intuition: Embracing the Unknown

Intuition is often described as a kind of knowing without knowing—a sense of clarity or understanding that arises without conscious thought or reasoning. It may feel like a gut feeling, a hunch, or even a sudden flash of insight. It transcends logic, yet its truth can feel undeniable. But how do we differentiate between intuitive guidance and wishful thinking or fear-based reactions?

The key is to cultivate stillness—the ability to quiet the mind and become more attuned to the subtle whispers of our inner voice. In our fast-paced, logic-driven world, intuition is often drowned out by the constant noise of everyday life. But when we create space for silence—through meditation, mindfulness, or deep reflection—we begin to listen more closely to the wisdom that resides within.

There is also a spiritual element to intuition. It is not merely a mental or emotional process but is deeply connected to our higher self, our soul's knowing, and the universe's greater wisdom. When we align with our intuition, we enter a state of harmony with a larger, more expansive source of truth—one that transcends individual experience and taps into the collective consciousness. This is why intuitive insights often feel like revelations—truths that resonate deeply, even if we cannot fully explain them with logic.

Balancing Logic and Intuition: The Power of Duality

In life's journey, it is essential to find a balance between logic and intuition. Logic allows us to think critically, analyze, and make decisions based on reason. It provides structure and helps us navigate the practical aspects of life. Intuition, on the other hand, connects us to the mysteries of the unseen world, offering insights and wisdom that go beyond rational thought.

While it's easy to place logic on one side and intuition on the other, the most powerful way to live is by integrating both. We are meant to use logic to make informed decisions, set goals, and analyze situations, but we are also meant to trust our intuition to guide us when the logical path is unclear. Sometimes, logic alone can be limiting—or even paralyzing—especially when faced with uncertain decisions that don't have a clear-cut answer. In these moments, intuition can illuminate the way forward.

By embracing both sides of this duality, we can make more holistic, grounded decisions. The rational mind and intuitive wisdom can work in partnership, each supporting and informing the other. Logic helps us manifest our goals, while intuition leads us to opportunities that logic alone could never predict.

Navigating Confusion: Trusting Your Inner Guide

We all experience moments of confusion—times when life feels uncertain, the next step is unclear, or we feel lost in the vastness of possibilities. During these times, our intuitive guidance becomes especially valuable. When overwhelmed by fear, doubt, or indecision, it's easy to get caught in mental loops, trying to "figure everything out" with logic. But logic cannot always solve the deep existential questions that arise on the journey of life. It is in these moments that we must learn to trust the wisdom of our intuition.

When confusion arises, take a step back and breathe. Create space to clear your mind, whether through meditation, deep breathing, or a quiet walk. Allow your intuition to rise to the surface. Often, the answer won't come immediately, and that's okay. Trust the process of unfolding— sometimes, the guidance we seek arrives quietly, in its own time, when we are ready to receive it.

Intuition doesn't always give us the whole picture. Sometimes, it only offers the next step. Trust that once you take action, the path will become clearer. Intuition is a step-by-step process, guiding us slowly toward our highest good, even when the full journey isn't immediately visible.

The Role of Intuition in Relationships

One of the most powerful ways intuition manifests in our lives is in the context of relationships. Intuition guides us toward deeper understanding and connection with others, helping us sense hidden truths, unspoken needs, or potential conflicts. In relationships, intuition acts as a bridge between the conscious and unconscious mind, allowing us to navigate the subtleties of communication and connection.

Whether in romantic partnerships, friendships, or professional relationships, trusting your intuition can deepen your understanding of others and help you create more harmonious connections. For example, you may sense when someone is upset or when there's an underlying issue that hasn't been addressed. By listening to these intuitive nudges, you can approach relationships with greater empathy and awareness.

Intuition also serves as a guide in personal relationships—helping us know when to speak and when to remain silent, when to act and when to give space. Learning to trust your inner wisdom allows you to create authentic, balanced connections based on mutual understanding and respect.

Life Lesson: Embrace the Duality of Logic and Intuition

The life lesson here is to embrace the duality of logic and intuition, recognizing that both are essential to the journey of life. Intuition provides the wisdom we need to navigate the unknown, while logic helps us manifest our visions in the practical world. By cultivating the ability to trust both, we become more balanced, aligned, and capable of handling whatever life presents.

Practices to Strengthen Your Intuition:

1. Cultivate Mindfulness – Take time each day to sit in stillness and become aware of your thoughts and feelings. This helps you discern the subtle whispers of your intuition from the noise of everyday life.

2. Practice Deep Listening – The next time you feel uncertain, pause and check in with your intuition. Ask yourself: What is my gut telling me? What feels right in my heart? Trust your inner knowing, even if it doesn't always make logical sense.

3. Balance Rational Thinking with Intuitive Insights – When faced with a decision, balance analytical thinking with intuitive feelings. Reflect on both the facts and your instincts before making a choice.

4. Journaling for Clarity – Write down any intuitive insights you receive throughout the day. Use journaling as a tool to gain clarity on what your intuition is guiding you toward.

5. Trust the Timing – Intuitive guidance often unfolds in its own time. Sometimes, the answers we seek don't come immediately, but with patience and trust, they will arrive when we are ready.

Integrating Logic and Intuition

In your journey of life, intuition is one of your most powerful allies. By learning to listen to and trust your inner wisdom, you can navigate confusion, make empowered decisions, and live in greater alignment with your highest self.

The balance between logic and intuition is key—it is not about rejecting one for the other, but rather integrating both into a harmonious, empowered life. As you step forward on your journey, trust that the wisdom you seek is always within you, waiting to guide you through the unknown.

CHAPTER 4

NURTURING CREATION

Embracing the Flow of Abundance and Creativity

Life's journey is rich with the potential to create, nurture, and bring new ideas and experiences into being. Whether you are cultivating relationships, embarking on creative endeavors, or fostering personal growth, the energy of creation is always present—both around you and within you. Creation is not just about bringing physical things into existence; it's about fostering an environment in which new possibilities can thrive and evolve.

In this journey, we explore the deep, fertile energy of abundance, creativity, and nurturing—and how you can connect with these forces to manifest your desires.

To truly nurture creation, you must first understand that creativity and abundance are not limited resources. Rather, they are infinite forces of the universe, constantly flowing through you when you open yourself to them. Think of the Earth as a reflection of this energy—an abundant and fertile source that continually gives birth to new life. You, too, can tap into this universal flow of abundance by cultivating creativity and nurturing the seeds of your ideas with patience, love, and care.

The Energy of Nurturing: Connection to the Earth

Creation is often symbolized by the nurturing, life-giving energy of the Earth. Just as the Earth supports the growth of plants, animals, and all living things, we too must create an environment where our ideas and relationships can grow and flourish. The Earth's energy is grounded, steady, and filled with life—teaching us that creation requires patience, care, and a deep connection to the natural rhythms of life.

When you align yourself with the Earth's energy, you learn the art of nurturing what is important to you—whether it's a creative project, a relationship, a business idea, or your own emotional and spiritual growth. Just like a seed that is carefully planted, watered, and given sunlight, your creations need love, attention, and time to unfold.

To nurture creation in your own life, consider the following:

- Be Present – To nurture anything, you must be fully present with it. Whether it's a new idea, a relationship, or a personal goal, give it your undivided attention. Cultivate mindfulness in your actions, ensuring that you approach everything with care and intention.

- Provide Support – Nurturing creation is not just about effort but also about providing the right conditions for growth. Whether it's encouragement, education, resources, or emotional support, give your creations the space and nourishment they need to develop.

- Be Patient – Just like a plant takes time to grow, your creative projects and relationships require time to blossom. Don't rush the process—trust that growth happens at its own pace and unfolds naturally when the time is right.

Creativity: The Birth of New Ideas

Creativity is one of the most powerful forces we possess as humans. It is the ability to bring something new into existence—whether it's an art form, a solution to a problem, or a fresh perspective on life. Creativity is the spark of life itself—allowing us to evolve and adapt in our ever-changing world.

However, nurturing creativity requires us to remove barriers that block our creative potential. These barriers often include self-doubt, fear of failure, perfectionism, or external pressures. When we allow ourselves the freedom to create without expectation, we enter a flow state where ideas unfold naturally.

To nurture your creativity, practice the following:

- Create Space for Inspiration – Make time for creative exploration, whether through art, writing, problem-solving, or any form of self-expression. Explore different outlets and find what excites you.

- Let Go of Perfectionism – Creativity is about expression, not perfection. Don't be afraid to experiment and make mistakes—each mistake is an opportunity to learn.

- Trust the Process – Creativity doesn't always happen instantly. It may take time to find the right path or form. Be patient and trust that the process will unfold when you are ready.

- Collaborate and Share – Creativity often flourishes when shared with others. Collaborating with like-minded individuals can bring new perspectives and enhance your creative output.

Abundance: Creating Space for Prosperity and Growth

Abundance is not just about material wealth—it is a state of mind and energy that invites prosperity into all areas of life. It is about recognizing that there is more than enough—more love, more opportunities, more resources, and more joy.

The abundance mindset shifts you from a place of scarcity and limitation into one of possibility and growth.

Abundance is deeply tied to the act of nurturing. When you nurture something, whether it's an idea, a relationship, or your own well-being, you create a fertile ground for abundance to blossom. The key is to open yourself to the flow of abundance by maintaining an attitude of gratitude and trust. When you focus on what is working and what is growing in your life, you invite more of it to manifest.

To cultivate abundance, consider the following:

- Be Grateful – Gratitude is the key to unlocking abundance. When you appreciate what you have, you shift your focus from lack to flourishing, creating a positive vibration that attracts even more.

- Give Freely – Abundance flows when we share it with others. Whether it's your time, resources, love, or knowledge, giving creates a cycle of generosity that returns to you.

- Open Yourself to Possibility – Abundance is about seeing opportunities everywhere, not just in expected places. Be open to the unexpected, and trust that the universe will provide when you are ready.

Life Lesson: Nurture Creation in All Aspects of Life

The life lesson here is about nurturing the process of creation in all aspects of your life. Whether you're building a business, fostering a relationship, or bringing a creative project to life, the act of nurturing requires love, patience, attention, and trust.

Here are some practices to help you nurture creation:

1. Practice Self-Care – Nurture your own well-being so you can better nurture others. Take care of your body, mind, and spirit with healthy habits, self-compassion, and rest.

2. Cultivate Patience – Understand that growth takes time. Be patient with yourself and others as you nurture goals and relationships. Trust that everything unfolds in its own time.

3. Engage in Creative Expression – Regularly participate in activities that inspire creativity. Whether it's writing, painting, gardening, or any other outlet, make time for it.

4. Focus on Growth – Ask yourself daily: What can I nurture today? Shift your focus to developing your ideas, relationships, and personal growth.

5. Give and Receive Generously – Abundance flows when you both give and receive. Share your gifts, resources, and love, and be open to receiving them as well.

The Power of Nurturing Creation

By embracing the energy of nurturing creation, you align yourself with the abundance of the universe—cultivating creativity, prosperity, and joy in all aspects of life.

The act of nurturing is love in motion—the essence of creation itself. Whether through the care we offer a loved one, the support we give to a dream, or the attention we devote to our own growth, nurturing shapes the world. It is the energy that fuels transformation—the quiet force behind the evolution of ideas, relationships, and communities. Through nurturing, we not only give life but also become the conduit through which the universe expresses its boundless love and creativity.

CHAPTER 5

ESTABLISHING STRUCTURE AND AUTHORITY

Building Strong Foundations for Lasting Success

In the journey of life, there comes a point when creativity and spontaneity must be anchored in discipline and structure. Just as a tree requires strong roots to grow tall and steady, your ambitions and dreams need a solid foundation to flourish. Establishing structure and authority in your life means developing the discipline, responsibility, and leadership necessary to build a future that is not only successful but sustainable.

Creating structure doesn't mean rigidly controlling every aspect of life; rather, it involves setting up a framework that supports growth, stability, and achievement. It's about having a clear vision, setting purposeful goals, and putting in the necessary work to bring your dreams to fruition. Authority in this context is not about exerting power over others but about taking control of your own destiny and having the courage to lead yourself toward your goals. The masculine energy associated with this chapter represents strength, assertiveness, and the ability to act decisively in the face of challenges.

By embracing the energy of structure and authority, you create a life that reflects your true potential, grounded in the values of responsibility, consistency, and long-term vision.

The Power of Discipline and Structure

Discipline is the cornerstone of any great achievement. It is the ability to stay focused on your goals, even when distractions arise or the path becomes challenging. Structure, on the other hand, provides the framework that allows you to channel your energy productively. It brings clarity and organization, enabling you to take consistent, measured steps toward success.

When you establish structure in your life, you create an environment where your dreams can take root and grow. This means setting clear goals, developing routines that align with those goals, and implementing systems that keep you on track. Without structure, it's easy to get lost in the chaos of life and feel overwhelmed by the sheer volume of possibilities. However, with the right structure, you can channel your energy effectively, stay focused, and move forward with confidence.

To establish structure in your life, consider the following:

- Create a Plan: Begin by setting clear, actionable goals. What do you want to achieve in the short term and long term? Break these goals down into manageable tasks and create a timeline for achieving them.

- Develop Consistent Routines: Establish daily habits that support your goals. Consistency is key to maintaining progress. Whether it's setting aside time each day for focused work, exercise, or reflection, daily routines help reinforce your commitment to your vision.

- Prioritize and Organize: Learn to prioritize your tasks based on importance and urgency. Organizing your time, space, and resources reduces unnecessary stress and ensures you are consistently moving toward your objectives.

Leadership and Personal Authority

Leadership isn't just about guiding others—it starts with leading yourself. Personal authority is the ability to take responsibility for your actions and decisions and to lead your life with clarity and intention. When you develop personal authority, you stop seeking external validation or permission and instead trust yourself to make decisions that align with your values and goals.

To establish true leadership in your life, begin by owning your choices and embracing responsibility. This means acknowledging your role in your own successes and challenges and understanding that you have the power to change the course of your life at any moment.

A key element of leadership is knowing when to take initiative and when to delegate. If you're leading others, this balance is crucial. However, when leading yourself, it's important to recognize your own strengths and weaknesses and take charge of what you can control.

To develop leadership and personal authority:

- Trust Yourself: Develop confidence in your decision-making abilities. Trust your instincts and know that your judgment is valid. When you trust yourself, others will also begin to trust you.

- Own Your Responsibility: Acknowledge that your life and outcomes are shaped by the choices you make. Take responsibility for both your successes and your failures, and learn from each experience.

- Set Boundaries: Healthy leadership requires boundaries. Learn to say no when necessary, protect your time and energy, and ensure that you are prioritizing your well-being and goals.

The Masculine Energy of Creation

The masculine energy explored in this chapter represents strength, action, and assertiveness. It is the energy that drives you to act on your goals, take the necessary steps toward success, and stand tall in the face of adversity. It is the force that pushes you to establish discipline and structure and to take command of your life.

In today's world, masculine energy is often associated with external power, competition, and success. However, true masculine energy is about inner strength and the ability to create with purpose. It is about having the courage to act decisively, take calculated risks, and honor your own authority.

To harness masculine energy, consider the following:

- Be Assertive: Learn to assert your needs and desires in a way that is respectful to yourself and others. Stand firm in your values, and do not shy away from taking bold actions when necessary.

- Take Action: Masculine energy is action-oriented. Don't wait for the perfect moment—take the first step toward your goals and continue moving forward with determination.

- Be Consistent: Consistency is a hallmark of masculine energy. Like the steady, reliable force of a river, you can create lasting change through persistent effort. Stay committed to your goals and keep pushing forward, even when the road gets tough.

Life Lesson: Embrace Responsibility and Set Long-Term Goals

The life lesson is simple yet profound: Take responsibility for your life, set long-term goals, and establish the discipline to create a solid foundation for your future. Without responsibility, there can be no true freedom. By embracing your role as the creator of your own reality, you empower yourself to build a life that reflects your deepest desires and potential.

Consider the following practices to embrace responsibility and structure in your life:

1. Set Clear Long-Term Goals: Define what you want to achieve in the next 5, 10, or even 20 years. Think about your career, relationships, personal growth, and contributions to the world. Break down these long-term goals into smaller, actionable steps.

2. Create Systems for Success: Develop systems and routines that help you stay on track. These could include time-management techniques, budgeting practices, or personal development rituals that align with your goals.

3. Commit to Consistent Action: Action is key. Commit to taking consistent steps toward your goals, even if they are small at first. Every action builds momentum, and over time, your efforts will compound into significant progress.

4. Cultivate Inner Strength: The more you trust in your abilities and take responsibility for your actions, the better you'll handle life's challenges with resilience. Cultivate a mindset that embraces challenges as opportunities for growth.

5. Lead with Integrity: Whether you're leading yourself or others, lead with integrity and clarity. Let your actions reflect your values, and take pride in knowing that your leadership is rooted in authenticity and purpose.

By establishing structure and embracing personal authority, you create a solid foundation for a life of lasting success. Responsibility, discipline, and leadership are not burdens but keys to unlocking your full potential. When you harness the masculine energy of action and assertiveness, you can step confidently into your future, knowing that every goal—big or small—is within your reach. Structure is the framework within which you build your dreams, and authority is the strength that carries them through.

CHAPTER 6

SEEKING SPIRITUAL WISDOM

The Pursuit of Higher Knowledge and Spiritual Growth

In our life's journey, there comes a time when we seek something deeper than the material world—a need for spiritual guidance, wisdom, and a greater understanding of our place in the universe. This journey is about seeking spiritual wisdom, exploring traditional teachings, and remaining open to the evolution of our own beliefs. It's about embracing the path of higher knowledge and recognizing that true wisdom often comes from both study and personal experience.

The pursuit of spiritual wisdom is a lifelong journey, one that invites us to remain curious, humble, and receptive to the lessons life has to offer. It calls us to connect with something greater than ourselves, seek guidance from those who have walked the path before us, and continuously grow in understanding. Along the way, we may encounter various philosophies, religions, and spiritual practices, each offering unique insights and tools for navigating the mysteries of existence.

However, the wisdom we gain is not static—it is a living, evolving understanding that adapts and expands as we grow. Spiritual wisdom helps us align with our true purpose, understand our inner selves, and navigate life with a deeper sense of peace and meaning.

Exploring Tradition and Spiritual Teachings

For centuries, human beings have sought answers to life's biggest questions: Why are we here? What is the purpose of suffering? How can we find peace? Spiritual teachings from various traditions provide insights into these questions. These teachings often come in the form of sacred texts, philosophies, rituals, and practices designed to help us connect with the divine, understand ourselves, and live a life of virtue and wisdom.

While traditional teachings have stood the test of time, it's important to approach them with an open mind and heart. The essence of spiritual wisdom is not confined to any one tradition but rather lies in the universal truths they share: love, compassion, purpose, and the pursuit of higher consciousness. When seeking spiritual wisdom, allow yourself to explore the richness of various traditions, from ancient wisdom to contemporary practices, while remaining discerning about what resonates with your soul.

To seek spiritual wisdom, consider the following practices:

- Study Sacred Texts: Engage with spiritual books, sacred writings, and teachings that have inspired generations. Whether it's the Bible, the Bhagavad Gita, the Tao Te Ching, or more modern spiritual works, these texts provide valuable insights into the nature of life and the human experience.

- Attend Spiritual Gatherings: Whether it's a traditional church service, a meditation group, or a community focused on personal growth, gathering with others on a similar spiritual path can be incredibly enriching. Listening to others' experiences and insights helps you see the larger picture and deepens your understanding.

- Seek Out Mentors and Teachers: Find spiritual mentors, teachers, or guides who can help illuminate your path. A mentor provides perspective, shares wisdom from their own journey, and offers guidance for navigating life's challenges—not just from books but from lived experience.

The Importance of Mentorship and Guidance

Throughout history, every spiritual tradition has emphasized the role of the teacher or mentor. Whether sages, gurus, shamans, or spiritual guides, mentors provide us with the tools to access higher wisdom. They help refine our understanding of the sacred, offer guidance on living a moral and meaningful life and encourage us when our path becomes unclear.

However, it is important to remember that true mentorship fosters spiritual independence. While mentors provide guidance, they also encourage you to connect with your own inner wisdom and cultivate your relationship with the divine. They help you see that the answers you seek are already within you, even as they offer their support and wisdom.

To invite mentorship into your spiritual journey, consider the following:

- Being Open to Guidance: Seek out spiritual teachers or mentors who resonate with your journey. This may take the form of a formal teacher-student relationship or simply finding those whose wisdom inspires you—whether in person, through books, podcasts, or online communities.

- Asking the Right Questions: A mentor can guide you to ask deeper questions about your own life and soul's purpose. What do you truly believe? What is your calling? How do you navigate the unknown? These questions can lead to profound insights.

- Embracing the Teacher Within: Your greatest mentor is often your own inner wisdom. Learning to listen to your intuition, reflect on your experiences, and trust your inner guidance allows you to evolve spiritually in ways no one else can dictate.

Allowing Your Beliefs to Evolve

Spiritual wisdom is not a one-size-fits-all concept. As you grow, your beliefs will likely evolve, and this is a natural and healthy part of the journey. Just as we physically grow and change, our spiritual understanding deepens and adapts. At different points in life, you may feel drawn to different spiritual paths or traditions. The key is to remain open to change and allow your beliefs to evolve as you learn and experience more.

Embracing the evolution of your beliefs means allowing yourself the space to question, explore, and shift your perspective. What you once believed may not serve you in the same way as you grow—and that's okay. Spiritual growth is about expansion, not stagnation.

Consider these practices to allow your beliefs to evolve:

- Question with Curiosity: Don't be afraid to ask questions about your beliefs. Why do you believe what you believe? Is this belief empowering you or limiting you? Challenge your assumptions and seek deeper understanding.

- Stay Open to New Experiences: Life has a way of presenting new perspectives and opportunities for growth. Stay open to new spiritual practices, teachings, or philosophies that resonate with you. You don't need to discard everything you've learned—rather, integrate new insights into your current understanding.

- Trust the Process: Spiritual growth doesn't happen overnight. Trust that your beliefs will evolve naturally as you encounter new experiences, meet new people, and explore different teachings. Know that every step of the journey is part of your unique path.

Life Lesson: Continuously Seek Wisdom, Allowing Space for Growth

The life lesson is to seek wisdom continuously while allowing space for your understanding to evolve as you grow. Spiritual growth is not about arriving at a final answer but about remaining open to the journey itself. Every step on your spiritual path brings you closer to the truth of who you are, and the more you seek, the more you will find.

Remember, the pursuit of wisdom is an ongoing journey. Allow yourself to evolve spiritually as you encounter new experiences, meet new people, and explore new practices. Be patient with yourself and trust that your path will unfold in its own time.

To embrace this lesson:

1. Engage in Lifelong Learning: Spiritual wisdom is a lifelong pursuit. Keep learning—whether through books, meditation, classes, or conversations with others. Every experience holds the potential for growth.

2. Trust the Process of Evolution: Understand that your spiritual beliefs may change over time. This is a sign of growth, not failure. Allow your understanding to deepen and expand as you continue your journey.

3. Honor the Teachers Along the Way: Recognize that mentors and teachers are an integral part of the journey. Be open to their guidance, but also remember that your own inner wisdom is the ultimate teacher.

By seeking spiritual wisdom, you connect with the deeper truths of existence, finding peace, purpose, and guidance on your journey. Whether through formal teachings or inner revelations, spiritual wisdom provides the compass to navigate life's mysteries with clarity and grace.

CHAPTER 7

HARMONY AND RELATIONSHIPS

Building Meaningful Connections and Nurturing Harmony

Life is built on relationships—whether with family, friends, colleagues, or romantic partners. Relationships provide us with support, joy, challenges, and opportunities for growth. They shape our experiences and teach us valuable lessons about ourselves and the world around us. The key to fulfilling relationships lies in cultivating harmony, balance, and conscious choice. Every connection we make has the potential to shape our lives in profound ways, and through relationships, we often learn our most significant life lessons.

Partnerships are at the heart of our existence—personal, professional, or spiritual. Our relationships with others reflect our inner state, and the harmony or discord we experience in our connections often mirrors the balance or imbalance within ourselves. Life encourages us to view relationships not just as external interactions but as reflections of our own emotional and spiritual landscape. By fostering self-love, balance, and conscious choices, we can create connections that not only serve us but also contribute to our overall sense of peace and fulfillment.

The Importance of Conscious Choices in Relationships

Every relationship we form is an expression of who we are at that moment in time. Our choices—the way we communicate, the boundaries we set, and the energy we bring—shape the dynamics of our connections. Conscious relationships are those in which both parties are actively aware of the energy they exchange, the needs they express, and the values they uphold.

In any meaningful connection, it's important to make intentional decisions about how you engage. Are you showing up as your authentic self? Are you choosing to love and support others with an open heart? Are you *mindful* of *how* your actions, words, and energy influence those around you? Conscious choices mean being aware of how you interact and ensuring that your actions align with your values and desires.

Relationships built on awareness and intention are more likely to flourish. These connections are not based on unconscious patterns or reactive behavior but on mutual respect, clear communication, and shared goals. By consciously choosing the people you surround yourself with and actively participating in the growth of these relationships, you create a foundation of trust and understanding.

The Role of Self-Love in Healthy Relationships

Self-love is the foundation of all healthy relationships. Before we can truly love and care for others, we must first love and care for ourselves. When we nurture our inner selves—through self-compassion, healthy boundaries, and self-acceptance—we bring more love and balance into our connections with others.

Self-love means understanding your worth, accepting your flaws, and prioritizing your needs. It involves taking the time to care for your emotional and mental well-being and setting boundaries that protect your peace. When we love ourselves, we are less likely to enter relationships that drain us or take advantage of our energy. Instead, we attract relationships that honor us, that are balanced, and that support our growth.

Practicing self-love involves:

- Taking Care of Yourself: Prioritize your physical, emotional, and spiritual needs. Rest when needed, nourish your body with healthy food, and make time for activities that bring you joy.

- Setting Healthy Boundaries: Know your limits and be firm in protecting your personal space and emotional energy. Boundaries are not walls but guidelines that allow you to engage with others in a respectful and balanced way.

- Accepting Yourself: Embrace both your strengths and imperfections. Recognize that you are worthy of love and respect just as you are. Self-love is not about perfection but about acceptance and self-compassion.

When you cultivate self-love, you can bring that love into your relationships with others, creating connections that are nurturing, supportive, and enriching for everyone involved.

The Power of Harmony in Relationships

At the heart of every successful relationship is harmony—a state of balance, peace, and alignment between individuals. Harmony is the delicate dance of giving and receiving, of understanding and being understood. When we seek harmony in relationships, we prioritize mutual respect, emotional balance, and shared growth.

To foster harmony in relationships:

- Communicate Openly and Honestly: One of the key pillars of harmony is clear and open communication. Speak your truth, but also listen. Creating an environment where both parties feel heard and understood builds a foundation of trust and respect.

- Embrace Compromise and Flexibility: Harmony is not about control or rigid expectations but about finding middle ground. In relationships, it's important to be flexible, let go of the need to be right, and be willing to meet others halfway.

- Celebrate Differences: True harmony arises when we recognize that our differences are valuable. Instead of seeking to change others, we can learn from the diverse perspectives they bring to the relationship. Embrace individuality and find ways to celebrate those differences in your interactions.

When both parties contribute to the harmony of a relationship, it becomes a source of mutual enrichment, personal growth, and joy.

Balance in All Relationships

Whether with a romantic partner, a family member, a friend, or a colleague, balance is essential. Relationships that lack balance can quickly become draining or unhealthy. Balance involves giving and receiving in equal measure, supporting each other's growth, and respecting each other's needs.

In any relationship, it's important to assess whether both people are contributing equally to the emotional, mental, and physical well-being of the partnership. Are both people equally invested? Are both taking responsibility for their actions and feelings? Balance doesn't mean everything is always equal, but it does mean there is a mutual sense of respect and consideration.

Creating balance in relationships requires:

- Mutual Respect: Honor each other's feelings, thoughts, and boundaries.

- Equal Effort: Both individuals should be invested in maintaining the relationship, whether through time, effort, or emotional support.

- Acknowledging Differences: Recognize that differences in opinion, experience, and perspective are natural, and find ways to integrate those differences in a healthy way.

Life Lesson: Foster Conscious Relationships and Seek Balance

The life lesson is to foster conscious relationships—seeking balance, harmony, and self-love as a foundation for healthy connections. Our relationships are mirrors of our inner world. The more we cultivate balance and self-love within ourselves, the more harmonious our relationships become. By embracing our authentic selves and making conscious choices, we create the space for deeper, more meaningful connections.

Remember:

1. Make Conscious Choices: Be aware of the energy you bring to your relationships. Choose to engage in ways that reflect love, respect, and understanding.

2. Nurture Self-Love: Prioritize your well-being and ensure that you have a solid foundation of self-love before fully giving to others.

3. Create Harmony: Seek peace and balance in all your connections, fostering an environment of mutual respect and growth.

As you journey through life, the relationships you form will be among the most profound experiences of your existence. By cultivating conscious, harmonious, and balanced connections, you create a foundation for both personal and collective growth.

CHAPTER 8

TRIUMPH THROUGH DETERMINATION

The Power of Willpower, Perseverance, and Focus

In life, challenges are inevitable. They test our resilience, push our limits, and challenge our convictions. Yet within each obstacle lies an opportunity for growth, strength, and triumph. Life is about harnessing the transformative power of determination and willpower—understanding that perseverance can lead us to victory even in the face of adversity.

To triumph through determination, we must cultivate the strength to stay focused, keep moving forward, and overcome the hurdles along our path. Whether personal, professional, or spiritual, every challenge we face can become a stepping stone toward greater success and self-discovery. Victory is not just about achieving a goal—it is about the persistence and unwavering resolve required to reach that goal, regardless of the difficulties encountered along the way.

The Power of Willpower

Willpower is the internal force that drives us to take action despite obstacles, fatigue, or discouragement. It is the ability to stay committed to a goal and continue working toward it, even when the path is difficult or uncertain. Willpower is an essential component of success—it is the engine behind our persistence and the foundation of our personal strength.

At times, life presents challenges that seem insurmountable. In these moments, our willpower is tested the most. It is easy to feel tempted to give up, to surrender to the belief that things will never improve, or to accept defeat. However, willpower allows us to rise above those temptations, remain steady in the face of difficulty, and push forward toward our goals.

Developing willpower involves:

- Setting Clear Intentions: Know what you want to achieve and why it matters. Clarity of purpose strengthens your resolve and keeps you on track when distractions or difficulties arise.

- Staying Disciplined: Willpower requires discipline—the ability to consistently make choices that align with your long-term goals, even when short-term temptations or obstacles threaten your progress.

- Taking Small Steps: Willpower is not always about big, dramatic efforts; often, it's about the small, consistent actions you take every day. Breaking your goals into manageable steps makes the journey feel more achievable and provides frequent moments of progress to celebrate.

The Role of Perseverance in Overcoming Obstacles

Perseverance is the ability to keep moving forward despite setbacks. It is the quiet, steadfast commitment to a vision or goal, even when results seem delayed or the journey feels endless. Perseverance is what separates those who reach their goals from those who give up too soon. Success often comes not in one grand leap, but in many small, persistent steps.

There are times when the road to success will seem long and obstacles insurmountable. It's easy to feel discouraged when progress appears slow. But perseverance teaches us that the best rewards often require the most effort. Through perseverance, we learn to embrace the struggle, trusting that each challenge brings us closer to our ultimate goal.

To cultivate perseverance:

- Keep the End in Mind: When you feel weary or frustrated, reconnect with your vision. Remember why you started in the first place and keep your eyes on the prize.

- Embrace Setbacks as Lessons: Every setback offers valuable lessons. Instead of viewing obstacles as failures, see them as opportunities to learn, adapt, and refine your approach.

- Practice Patience: Success rarely happens overnight. Patience is crucial to perseverance. Trust that every effort you make moves you closer to your goal, even if the results aren't immediately visible.

Victory through Focus and Direction

Determination isn't just about grit—it's about having a clear focus and a sense of direction. Without focus, we can easily become distracted by the multitude of paths and opportunities that cross our way. To succeed, we must learn to say "no" to things that don't align with our goals and keep our energy and attention fixed on the most important tasks.

Focus is the skill of maintaining clarity and precision in our actions. It is the ability to block out distractions and direct our energy toward what matters most. Without focus, determination becomes scattered and weak, dissipating like a leaf in the wind.

To enhance your focus and direction:

- Prioritize Your Goals: Identify the most important objectives in your life and work toward them first. Focus on what truly matters, and let go of activities or projects that dilute your energy.

- Set Specific Milestones: Break your journey into smaller, achievable goals. This provides direction and a sense of progress as you move forward.

- Minimize Distractions: Create an environment that supports your focus. Whether it's reducing social media exposure, finding a quiet workspace, or setting aside specific times for important work, minimizing distractions helps you maintain energy on what truly matters.

The Power of Inner Strength

Inner strength is not just about physical endurance—it is the ability to remain emotionally and mentally strong in the face of difficulties. It is the capacity to maintain your peace of mind, sense of self, and confidence, no matter the circumstances. When life challenges you, inner strength keeps you grounded, allowing you to respond with wisdom rather than react impulsively.

To strengthen your inner resolve:

- Cultivate Self-Belief: Trust in your ability to overcome obstacles. Self-doubt weakens your resolve, while self-belief empowers you to take decisive action.

- Stay Calm Under Pressure: Life will throw unexpected difficulties your way. The key to overcoming them is not to react impulsively but to respond thoughtfully and with poise.

- Take Care of Yourself: Emotional strength is supported by physical and mental well-being. Ensure you are taking care of your body and mind so that you can maintain resilience in the face of adversity.

Life Lesson: Triumph Through Determination

Stay focused on your goals and push through challenges with determination and inner strength. Life will inevitably present obstacles, but our ability to persevere, remain determined, and maintain focus determines our success. True victory is not found in avoiding difficulties but in facing them head-on with the confidence that we will overcome them.

Remember:

1. Willpower is Your Inner Force: It is the strength to keep going when everything inside you wants to quit. Stay clear about your intentions and move forward with discipline.

2. Perseverance Brings Growth: Success is built through persistence. Learn from every setback and keep pushing toward your goal with resilience.

3. Focus and Direction are Key: Keep your attention on what truly matters and eliminate distractions that lead you astray.

4. Inner Strength Powers You: Cultivate the inner resolve to face challenges with a calm and focused mind.

In the journey of life, determination is the force that propels us forward. With focus, perseverance, and a strong sense of inner resolve, you will triumph over every obstacle that comes your way. The path may be difficult, but the rewards—victory, growth, and fulfillment—are worth every step.

CHAPTER 9

INNER FORTITUDE AND COURAGE

Cultivating Courage, Resilience, and Compassion

In the face of life's challenges, we are often called to tap into a deeper well of strength than we even know we have. Inner fortitude is the quiet power that arises from within, enabling us to confront life's trials with courage, resilience, and an open heart. Life guides us to cultivate these qualities, teaching us how to master our internal fears and embrace our power through compassion—both for ourselves and for others.

True strength is not simply about physical endurance or mental toughness; it is about maintaining balance and peace during life's most trying moments. It means facing fear and uncertainty with the knowledge that, even in the darkest moments, we have the power to rise.

The Nature of Courage

Courage is not the absence of fear but the willingness to face it head-on. It is the strength to act despite uncertainty, doubt, or vulnerability. It takes courage to step out of our comfort zones, face the unknown, and confront challenges that seem insurmountable.

Many people mistakenly believe that courage is a rare or extraordinary trait, reserved only for heroes or those who perform grand acts. However, courage exists within every one of us. It appears in both big and small moments—choosing to speak our truth, standing up for what we believe in, taking a leap of faith in a new endeavor, or enduring difficult moments with grace and patience.

To cultivate courage:

- Face Your Fears: Instead of running from fear, walk directly toward it. Facing what scares us allows us to reclaim our power and proves that we can handle whatever life throws our way.

- Challenge Your Comfort Zone: True courage grows when we push beyond familiar boundaries. Seek out new challenges that stretch your limits and foster growth.

- Act in Spite of Fear: Fear is a natural response to uncertainty. Don't wait for fear to disappear—act anyway. Often, courage is demonstrated not in the absence of fear but in the willingness to move forward despite it.

Resilience: Bouncing Back Stronger

Resilience is the ability to recover from adversity. It allows us to endure difficult situations, rebound from setbacks, and emerge stronger. Life will inevitably place obstacles in our path—loss, disappointment, failure, or hardship—but our resilience determines how we respond to these challenges.

Resilience is not about avoiding pain or hardship; it is about how we rebuild ourselves after difficult moments. It means finding strength in vulnerability, learning from struggles, and allowing ourselves to heal and grow.

To cultivate resilience:

- Accept Life's Impermanence: Understand that nothing in life is permanent—not the good times nor the bad. Change is the only constant, and learning to accept it helps build emotional resilience.

- Find the Lesson in Pain: Every setback offers an opportunity for growth. When we learn from mistakes or difficulties, we transform pain into wisdom.

- Stay Connected to Your Inner Strength: Resilience comes from knowing that, no matter what life throws your way, you have the capacity to recover and move forward. Stay grounded in your self-belief.

- Take Care of Yourself: Resilience requires a strong foundation. Nurture your physical, emotional, and mental well-being so you have the resources to draw on during tough times.

Compassion: The Power of Inner Strength

At the heart of true strength is compassion—not just for others, but also for ourselves. Compassion is often seen as a soft and gentle quality, but in reality, it is one of the most powerful forces for personal growth and transformation. To be compassionate means to extend kindness and understanding, both outwardly and inwardly.

When life becomes difficult, it's easy to be hard on ourselves. We may feel shame for our perceived weaknesses, guilt for not doing better, or frustration with our limitations. However, self-compassion is the key to emotional healing and inner peace. By treating ourselves with the same patience and kindness that we offer others, we build a foundation of self-love that helps us navigate life's storms with grace.

To cultivate compassion:

- Practice Self-Kindness: Be gentle with yourself. When you make a mistake or face a setback, speak to yourself as you would a dear friend—with empathy and encouragement, not judgment.

- Let Go of Perfectionism: Understand that perfection is an illusion. Embrace your flaws and imperfections as part of your unique human experience.

- Extend Compassion to Others: Strength is also reflected in how we treat others. By approaching people with kindness, understanding, and patience, we uplift not only them but also ourselves.

- Forgive Yourself and Others: Forgiveness is a powerful form of compassion. Let go of resentment, guilt, or anger—holding onto these emotions only weakens your resilience and inner peace.

The Connection Between Courage, Resilience, and Compassion

Courage, resilience, and compassion are interconnected qualities that together form the foundation of inner strength. Courage allows us to face life's challenges, resilience helps us bounce back from hardship, and compassion nurtures our emotional well-being as we navigate our personal journey.

True inner strength is found when we can stand tall in the face of adversity, embrace our vulnerabilities, and move forward with both strength and kindness. We do not need to be invincible, nor do we need to be perfect. The essence of inner fortitude is recognizing that strength does not come from a lack of fear or pain but from our ability to endure, to rise after a fall, and to continue walking our path with a compassionate heart.

Life Lesson: True Strength Comes from Within

The life lesson of this chapter is simple yet profound: true strength comes from within. Build your inner resilience by confronting your fears, embracing setbacks as opportunities for growth, and extending compassion to yourself and others.

In moments of challenge:

- Draw on your courage: Face the situation head-on, knowing you have the power to navigate it.

- Lean into your resilience: Trust that you can bounce back from hardship and that the struggle itself is part of your growth.

- Be compassionate: Treat yourself with kindness and patience, and extend that same grace to others.

By cultivating courage, resilience, and compassion, you will develop a deep well of inner strength capable of withstanding any storm. This strength will not only help you survive but also allow you to thrive—transforming challenges into opportunities for growth, self-discovery, and transformation.

Remember, your greatest power lies in your ability to stand firm in your truth and rise with grace, no matter the trials you face.

CHAPTER 10

REFLECTION AND INNER WISDOM

Embracing Solitude and Uncovering Spiritual Truths

In the hustle and bustle of modern life, it's easy to get caught up in the noise and distractions around us. Yet, some of the most profound insights and personal growth emerge from moments of solitude and introspection. By embracing reflection, we open a path to discovering our inner wisdom and spiritual truths. Through deep introspection and quiet moments alone, we can uncover the hidden messages our soul is trying to communicate, aligning ourselves with a deeper understanding of life's mysteries.

Reflection is the practice of looking inward—taking time to contemplate experiences, emotions, and actions. It involves creating a quiet space to listen to your inner voice and make sense of the journey you've traveled. In this space, you can connect with the deeper aspects of yourself—the part that is not influenced by external opinions or distractions but speaks from a place of spiritual truth and self-awareness.

The Power of Solitude

Solitude is often misunderstood. In a world that values constant connectivity, being alone can sometimes feel uncomfortable or even undesirable. However, solitude is not about isolation or loneliness; it is about reconnecting with your true self. It provides the quiet space necessary for self-reflection, allowing you to hear your inner voice more clearly and connect with the spiritual truths that guide you.

In solitude, you step away from the noise of the world and tune in to what lies beneath the surface of your thoughts. This is where you begin to uncover your deepest wisdom—the insights that shape your actions, beliefs, and decisions. Solitude creates the space for healing and growth, and it is in these moments that you may gain clarity about what truly matters in your life.

To embrace solitude:

- Create Sacred Space: Find a quiet, peaceful place where you can be undisturbed. Whether it's a cozy corner in your home, a park, or a meditation room, make this space a sanctuary for introspection.

- Set Aside Time for Reflection: Just as you schedule appointments and commitments, prioritize solitude. Set aside moments each day or week to be alone with your thoughts and reflect on your experiences.

- Practice Mindfulness: Engage in mindfulness practices such as deep breathing, journaling, or meditation to enhance your ability to connect with your inner world.

Deep Introspection: Uncovering Spiritual Truths

Introspection is the act of turning inward to examine your thoughts, emotions, and motivations. It is an ongoing process of self-exploration and deeper understanding. Through introspection, you can begin to uncover spiritual truths—insights that go beyond the surface and reveal your true nature. These truths often emerge when you create space for silence and reflection, and they have the power to transform your perspective on life.

During moments of introspection, you may uncover hidden desires, unresolved emotions, or deeply held beliefs that you were previously unaware of. This is a powerful process of self-discovery and spiritual growth, leading to profound transformation. The more you reflect, the more clearly you can hear the wisdom of your inner self and align with your higher purpose.

To practice introspection:

- Ask Deep Questions: Start by asking yourself meaningful questions such as, "What am I seeking in my life?" or "What do I truly value?" These questions open doors to deeper understanding.

- Journal Your Thoughts: Writing down your reflections is a powerful way to clarify your inner world. Use a journal to explore your feelings, experiences, and lessons learned. This process can help you uncover wisdom and spiritual insights hidden beneath daily thoughts.

- Listen to Your Intuition: In moments of introspection, your intuition often speaks more clearly. Trust your inner guidance—it carries the wisdom of your soul and offers valuable insights from deep within.

Spiritual Growth Through Reflection

Spiritual growth is a continuous journey of self-discovery, healing, and alignment with your higher self. It requires a commitment to introspection and self-awareness. Reflection allows you to recognize patterns in your life, identify areas for growth, and tap into the deeper meaning of your experiences. Through this process, you move closer to your higher purpose and create a life that reflects your true values and beliefs.

Reflection also cultivates inner peace and clarity. As you delve into your inner world, you begin to recognize the interconnectedness of all things, developing a greater sense of spiritual understanding. This understanding doesn't come from external sources—it emerges from within, shaped by your own experiences, thoughts, and reflections.

To support spiritual growth:

- Practice Meditation: Meditation is a powerful tool for quieting the mind and connecting with inner wisdom. Even a few minutes each day can help you gain clarity and deepen spiritual awareness.

- Seek Guidance: While introspection is a personal journey, seeking guidance from spiritual teachers or mentors can provide valuable insights. Learning from others who have walked a similar path can expand your perspective and wisdom.

- Trust the Process: Spiritual growth doesn't happen overnight. Be patient with yourself and trust that each step of your journey contributes to the greater unfolding of your life's purpose.

Life Lesson: Embrace Solitude to Reconnect with Your Inner Self

The life lesson here is to embrace solitude as a vital tool for spiritual growth and self-discovery. When you create space for introspection, you reconnect with your inner wisdom, uncover deeper truths about your purpose, and align your life with your higher self.

Key Takeaways:

- Value Your Alone Time: Solitude is not a burden—it is a gift. Use this time wisely to reflect, meditate, and listen to the messages that arise from within.

- Trust Your Inner Guidance: Your inner wisdom is a compass that can navigate life's challenges. Trust it to lead you toward clarity, peace, and deeper understanding.

- Use Introspection for Growth: View introspection as a tool for spiritual and personal transformation. It allows you to release old patterns, heal past wounds, and align more fully with your true purpose.

By regularly engaging in introspection and embracing solitude, you tap into a wellspring of inner wisdom that fosters profound growth and spiritual awakening. In this space, you begin to realize that the answers you seek are already within you—you just need the courage to listen.

CHAPTER 11

CYCLES AND DESTINY

Embracing Life's Phases and Divine Timing

Life is not a straight path but rather a series of cycles, each bringing its own set of experiences, challenges, and opportunities. From the rhythms of the seasons to the stages of our personal growth, cycles shape the flow of our lives. Understanding and accepting that our journey unfolds according to divine timing allows us to move through these cycles with greater ease. Life moves through different phases—some of growth and expansion, others of rest and reflection—and each serves a unique purpose in our overall journey.

The energy of cycles is deeply connected to our understanding of destiny. Destiny is not a rigid, fixed outcome but rather an unfolding process—a series of moments and choices that lead us toward our highest potential. When we recognize that life is cyclical, we can move with its rhythms rather than resist them. This awareness teaches us that no matter where we are in our journey, we are exactly where we need to be.

The Cycles of Life: Embrace the Flow

Life is composed of a series of cycles—some long, some short, but all meaningful. These cycles are a natural part of existence and are reflected in the patterns of the seasons, the phases of the moon, and our personal experiences. Each cycle has its own distinct energy: some phases are about growth and expansion, while others are about rest, reflection, and preparation for what comes next.

A key aspect of these cycles is that they are always evolving. We do not experience constant growth, nor do we remain in one place forever. Just as the earth moves through cycles of planting, growing, and harvesting, so do we. At times, we undergo periods of intense growth, while at other times, we must retreat, reflect, and recharge before the next phase of action begins.

To embrace the flow of life's cycles:

- Recognize the season of your life: Are you in a season of growth, or are you in a time of rest and introspection? Identifying the cycle you're in helps you align with it rather than resist it.

- Accept periods of dormancy: Just as plants must go through winter to bloom in spring, there are times when rest and reflection are necessary for future growth. Embrace these moments of stillness as fertile ground for renewal.

- Honor the natural flow: Life does not require us to be "on" all the time. Understanding that life moves in phases allows you to recognize when it's time to push forward and when it's time to slow down.

Destiny: The Path Unfolding

Destiny is often misunderstood as a predetermined fate, but in reality, it is an unfolding journey. Each of us has a higher purpose, but the path to that purpose is rarely a straight line. Life's cycles guide us, showing us where we need to grow, what we need to learn, and when the right moment has come for us to take the next step.

While we cannot control everything that happens in our lives, we can trust that each moment has a purpose in our overall journey. Every experience—whether perceived as good or bad—contributes to the unfolding of our destiny. Destiny is not something to be feared; it is something to be embraced with trust and openness. By surrendering to the natural flow of life, we align more fully with our true purpose and step into our highest potential.

To understand and embrace your destiny:

- Trust the timing: Life unfolds according to divine timing. Even if it feels like things aren't happening fast enough, trust that everything is unfolding at the perfect moment.

- Look for signs and synchronicities: Life often guides us through subtle signs and synchronicities. Pay attention to patterns and messages—they may hold the keys to your destiny.

- Surrender control: While we all have agency in our lives, there are times when letting go and allowing life to unfold naturally can lead to greater fulfillment. Trust that you are being guided, even in moments of uncertainty.

The Rhythm of Change: Accepting Life's Phases

One of the most powerful lessons in understanding life's cycles is accepting that change is inevitable. There are periods of great expansion where everything seems to align, and growth feels effortless. There are also periods of contraction and reflection, where things may feel stagnant or uncertain. Instead of resisting these phases, we are invited to embrace them, knowing that each phase plays a vital role in our evolution.

Change can be uncomfortable, but it is through change that we grow. Just as a caterpillar must undergo a transformative period before becoming a butterfly, we, too, must go through cycles of transformation—shedding old habits, mindsets, and even identities. Approaching change with grace and patience is key to navigating life's cycles.

To embrace the rhythm of change:

- Accept the ebb and flow: Life is full of highs and lows. By embracing both, you free yourself from the pressure of trying to keep things the same. Every phase offers something valuable.

- Find wisdom in every phase: Whether you are in a season of success or challenge, there is always wisdom to be gained. Each cycle contributes to your growth in its own way.

- Trust that each phase has a purpose: Even if a phase feels difficult or confusing, remember that it is part of a greater picture. Every cycle brings you closer to a deeper understanding of yourself and the world around you.

Life Lesson: Trust the Rhythms of Life

The life lesson here is to accept the natural rhythms of life and trust that each phase—whether it's a time of growth or reflection—is essential to your journey. By recognizing that life moves in cycles, you can release the need for constant forward momentum and learn to embrace each phase with patience and trust.

Key Takeaways:

- Embrace the ebb and flow of life: Life is cyclical. Sometimes, we experience expansion, and other times, we go through contraction. Both are necessary for growth.

- Trust divine timing: Everything happens at the right time. Trust that the universe is guiding you and that you are exactly where you need to be.

- Find peace in uncertainty: Instead of resisting periods of uncertainty or challenge, embrace them as natural phases in your journey. Change is part of life, and it always leads to greater wisdom and growth.

Life moves in cycles, and each cycle serves a purpose. By accepting this truth and aligning with the natural flow of life, we can navigate our journey with grace, trust, and patience. Every phase holds its own gifts and lessons—embrace them, and you will find yourself moving more fluidly toward your destiny.

CHAPTER 12

BALANCE AND ACCOUNTABILITY

Living with Integrity and Recognizing the Impact of Our Actions

In the intricate dance of life, balance and accountability are essential for maintaining harmony and alignment with our true selves. Life is not just about achieving success or pursuing our dreams; it's also about how we navigate our relationships, actions, and choices. This journey explores the concepts of fairness, balance, and accountability, emphasizing the importance of understanding the karmic consequences of our actions. Every choice we make—whether big or small—creates a ripple effect, shaping not only our own lives but also the lives of those around us.

Balance is not simply about finding peace between opposing forces; it's about integrating these forces in a way that creates harmony. Accountability, on the other hand, involves taking responsibility for our actions, owning the consequences of our decisions, and learning from them. When we practice both balance and accountability, we align ourselves with the natural flow of life and the universe's laws.

Fairness: The Key to Harmonious Living

Fairness is a fundamental principle for maintaining balance in our lives and relationships. It's not just about treating others equally—it's about being just, honest, and making decisions that reflect integrity. Life often presents situations that require us to choose between competing interests, values, or perspectives. In these moments, fairness serves as the compass that guides us toward choices that honor not just our own needs but also the well-being of others.

To live a life of fairness:

- Evaluate situations from multiple perspectives: True fairness requires seeing beyond personal biases and considering the feelings, needs, and perspectives of others. Put yourself in others' shoes to make choices that benefit everyone, not just yourself.

- Make decisions based on integrity: Fairness is rooted in integrity. If a choice feels wrong or compromises your values, pause and reconsider. Living in alignment with your values is key to making just and ethical decisions.

- Recognize when unfairness occurs: Sometimes, unfairness is not obvious. Be aware of when you are being treated unfairly, but also reflect on whether you might be unintentionally contributing to imbalance or injustice. Being fair requires honesty with yourself as well as with others.

Karmic Accountability: Understanding the Impact of Your Actions

Every action we take has consequences, shaping not just our present but also our future experiences. This concept is often referred to as karma—the understanding that the energy we put into the world will eventually return to us. Karma is not a punishment but a universal law of cause and effect. It reminds us that the kindness, love, or negativity we give to others will, in some form, come back to us.

When we make choices with awareness and responsibility, we create positive karma. When we act without considering the consequences, we may attract situations that require us to learn hard lessons. Accountability means acknowledging the impact of our actions and using that awareness to create a better future.

To practice karmic accountability:

- Take responsibility for your actions: Whether big or small, taking responsibility is the first step in correcting mistakes. Avoid blame and judgment, as they hinder growth. Instead, own your choices and view them as opportunities for learning.

- Reflect on your choices: Regularly assess your decisions and their outcomes. Are you happy with the energy you've put into the world? Have your actions aligned with your values? If not, what changes can you make moving forward?

- Understand the law of cause and effect: Everything you do creates a ripple in the universe. Every thought, word, and action sets a wave in motion that eventually returns to you. By recognizing this, you can make more conscious decisions that align with your highest purpose.

Balance: Harmony Between Giving and Receiving

In addition to fairness and accountability, life requires a sense of balance. This balance involves both internal and external harmony—the balance between work and rest, giving and receiving, action and reflection. We often find ourselves caught between extremes, juggling responsibilities, desires, and relationships. However, maintaining balance is essential for long-term well-being and growth.

Balance is not something achieved once and maintained forever; it is an ongoing process of recalibration. Life is dynamic, and as circumstances change, so too must our approach to balance.

To cultivate balance in your life:

- Practice self-awareness: Pay attention to areas of your life that feel out of balance. Are you giving too much energy to work while neglecting your health or relationships? Or are you overindulging in comfort while avoiding responsibilities? By tuning in to your inner state, you can recognize imbalances before they escalate.

- Create boundaries: Boundaries are essential for maintaining balance. Learn to say "no" when necessary and protect your energy. Setting limits helps preserve your well-being and ensures you have the time and space to nurture yourself and others.

- Find harmony in relationships: Healthy relationships are built on mutual respect, fairness, and balance. Ensure that you are neither over-giving nor over-receiving. Strive for equality and mutual support, and recognize when imbalance arises so that you can address it with openness and honesty.

Life Lesson: Practice Fairness and Integrity

The life lesson in this chapter is to recognize the profound impact of every choice and action. Practicing fairness, honesty, and integrity in all aspects of life ensures that each decision you make ripples out positively into the world. The consequences of your actions—both positive and negative—shape your destiny, making it essential to approach every choice with awareness and responsibility.

- Own your choices: Your life is shaped by the choices you make. Take responsibility for both your successes and failures, knowing that each step is part of your journey of growth.

- Create balance: In every aspect of life, strive for balance—between work and rest, giving and receiving, personal growth and relationship growth. Balance is key to sustainability and long-term happiness.

- Learn from your mistakes: No one is perfect. Mistakes are inevitable, but the key is to learn from them, make amends if necessary, and use those lessons to grow into a more conscious and balanced person.

By practicing fairness, embracing accountability, and creating balance in all areas of life, you align yourself with the natural flow of the universe. Life becomes a journey of integrity and growth, where each decision you make is a step toward a more harmonious and fulfilling existence.

CHAPTER 13

SURRENDER AND PERSPECTIVE

The Power of Letting Go and Embracing a New Outlook

In our fast-paced, goal-oriented world, we often cling tightly to control, believing that peace can only be found by managing every outcome. However, life's true wisdom often lies in surrender—the act of releasing the need to control everything and trusting in the natural flow of life. The transformative power of surrender can shift our perspective, helping us grow spiritually, emotionally, and mentally.

Surrender does not mean giving up or abandoning our desires; rather, it is about letting go of rigid control and accepting that sometimes the universe has its own plans. Through patience and self-sacrifice, we learn to flow with life's currents instead of struggling against them. As we release our grip on what we think should happen, we create space for new perspectives, deeper clarity, and personal growth.

Letting Go of Control: The Path to Freedom

Control is a powerful illusion. While it may feel safe and empowering to direct every aspect of our lives, this illusion can also become a source of stress, anxiety, and frustration. The more we try to control outcomes, the more we limit the possibilities that life has to offer. By surrendering control, we free ourselves from the constant struggle to make things happen exactly as we envision, allowing life to unfold in its natural rhythm.

To embrace surrender:

- Accept uncertainty: Life is unpredictable, and control often provides only the illusion of certainty. Rather than fearing the unknown, embrace life's mystery. Trust that even when things don't unfold as planned, a greater purpose is at work.

- Release attachment to outcomes: It's natural to want things to go a certain way, but excessive attachment can prevent you from seeing the broader picture. Let go of rigid expectations and trust that whatever happens is part of your growth.

- Embrace flexibility: When you release control, you create space for spontaneity and adaptability. Life often presents unexpected opportunities, and surrendering allows you to be more receptive to these surprises.

Patience and Self-Sacrifice: The Art of Allowing

Surrender requires patience—the ability to wait without anxiety or frustration. It also involves a form of self-sacrifice, where we let go of our ego's desires and allow something greater than ourselves to guide us. Patience in this context is not passive waiting but an active trust in life's process. It is the wisdom that says, "I don't have to force things to happen; they will unfold in their own time."

To practice patience and self-sacrifice:

- Trust the timing of life: Everything has its time and place. Trust that the right people, opportunities, and circumstances will come into your life when the time is right. Your task is to stay aligned and ready when they do.

- Practice mindfulness in moments of waiting: Use periods of uncertainty to practice mindfulness. Instead of rushing ahead or trying to force an outcome, be present and observe. Often, the answers you seek appear when you least expect them.

- Surrender your ego's need for control: Self-sacrifice isn't about martyrdom—it's about setting aside your ego's attachment to specific outcomes and allowing your deeper wisdom (or the universe's flow) to guide you. The more you release control, the more space you create for insight and growth.

Shifting Perspective: Seeing Life with New Eyes

Sometimes, the greatest growth comes not from pushing forward but from stepping back and shifting perspective. When we release the need for control, we open ourselves to new ways of seeing things. Surrender allows us to move beyond the narrow lens through which we view our challenges and see them from a completely new angle.

A fresh perspective often brings clarity and wisdom that were previously obscured by fear, stress, or rigid thinking. It helps us realize that the difficulties we face may not be obstacles but rather opportunities for growth.

To shift your perspective:

- Pause and reflect: When you feel frustrated or overwhelmed, take a step back and reflect. Ask yourself: What might I be missing? Is there another way to view this challenge?

- Look for the lesson: Life constantly presents opportunities to learn and grow. Surrendering allows you to recognize these lessons, especially when you release attachment to specific outcomes. Shift your perspective by seeking wisdom in every experience.

- Embrace paradox: Life is full of contradictions—light and dark, joy and sorrow, success and failure. Shifting your perspective means recognizing the beauty and growth that arise from life's dualities. By accepting both sides, you gain a deeper understanding of yourself and your journey.

Life Lesson: Release Control and Embrace the Flow of Life

The key lesson here is to surrender the need for control and embrace life's natural fluidity. When we let go of rigid expectations, we open ourselves to unexpected lessons and blessings. The more we release our fear of uncertainty, the more we experience growth, joy, and wisdom. Surrendering isn't about giving up—it's about embracing the unknown with curiosity and trust.

- Let go of rigid expectations: Recognize when you're holding on too tightly to a certain outcome. Practice releasing these attachments and trust that life will provide what you need when the time is right.

- Cultivate patience: Learn to wait with trust and presence, knowing that the universe has its own timing. While waiting, focus on your personal growth and development.

- Shift your perspective: When faced with challenges, take a step back and search for the hidden lessons. Life is not always what it seems at first glance. Changing your viewpoint can open doors to new possibilities.

Ultimately, surrender is about creating the space to trust, allow, and grow. It teaches us that we don't have to force life into being; instead, we can step into its natural flow, knowing that we are part of something larger than ourselves. Through surrender and a shift in perspective, we align with life's rhythms, leading to greater peace, clarity, and wisdom on our journey.

CHAPTER 14

TRANSFORMATION AND RENEWAL

Embracing Change and Rebirth

Change is the one constant in life, yet it is often one of the hardest things to accept. The transition from one phase to another can stir up fear, resistance, and uncertainty, but it is precisely in these moments of transformation that we are truly reborn. Embrace endings as opportunities for profound change, signaling the beginning of a new cycle of growth, healing, and renewal.

Transformation is not merely an event—it is a process, a journey requiring us to let go of the past and step into the unknown with courage. This chapter teaches that endings are not losses but essential moments in our evolution. With every ending comes the potential for a new beginning, a chance to renew ourselves and move forward with fresh eyes, new energy, and greater clarity.

Embracing Endings: The Gift of Closure

Every phase of life carries with it an inevitable end. Whether it's the conclusion of a relationship, the closing of a chapter in your career, or the shifting of your internal landscape, endings are a natural part of life's cycle. Often, we resist endings because they bring feelings of grief, loss, or uncertainty. However, endings are not to be feared—they are seeds of transformation.

To embrace endings:

- Release attachment: Often, the hardest part of transformation is releasing what no longer serves us. The end of a relationship, career, or life phase can bring feelings of loss, but holding onto outdated situations prevents you from evolving. Letting go of the old makes space for the new.

- Honor the journey: Every ending carries wisdom. Before moving on, reflect on what that phase taught you. What lessons did you learn? How did you grow? Honor the growth from the experience and acknowledge its contribution to your evolution.

- Trust the process: Change often feels uncomfortable because it asks us to step into the unknown. Trust that endings are part of a larger, divinely orchestrated process of growth and transformation. Just as winter makes way for spring, one cycle's closing creates fertile ground for new beginnings.

Transformation: Rebirth and the Power of Change

Transformation is not always easy, but it is necessary for personal growth. Just as a caterpillar must break free from its cocoon to become a butterfly, we must sometimes break free from old identities, habits, and beliefs to evolve into the next version of ourselves. Transformation is a journey, a shedding of old layers, a rebirth of the spirit, and an opportunity to emerge stronger, wiser, and more aligned with our true purpose.

To embrace transformation:

- Accept discomfort: Growth requires change, and change can feel uncomfortable. Accept that transformation may not always be smooth or easy. Embrace the discomfort as a necessary part of the process, knowing that the rewards are worth the challenge.

- Release limiting beliefs: Often, transformation asks us to let go of beliefs or patterns that have held us back. These may include self-doubt, fear of failure, or feelings of unworthiness. Letting go of limiting thoughts allows us to open up to new possibilities.

- Step into the unknown: Transformation requires us to step into the unknown with faith and courage. Embrace the uncertainty that comes with change, knowing that you are guided toward something better. Trust the process of evolution, even when you cannot yet see the full picture.

Renewal: The Beginning of a New Cycle

With transformation comes renewal. After shedding the old, we enter a phase of rebirth, where new possibilities, ideas, and opportunities arise. Renewal is a return to vitality, a fresh perspective, and a new way of being in the world. It's an invitation to align with your higher purpose, move forward intentionally, and take action toward your new vision.

To embrace renewal:

- Welcome new opportunities: Renewal is a time of fresh starts and new opportunities. Don't shy away from stepping into the next phase of your life. Whether it's a new job, a new relationship, or a new project, remain open to what comes your way.

- Create new intentions: As you embrace renewal, set goals or intentions aligned with your transformed self. Reflect on what you truly want to create in this new cycle, and take action toward making it a reality.

- Live with intention: The energy of renewal offers a powerful opportunity to live more consciously. Now that you have shed old patterns and embraced change, set your intentions clearly, and live in alignment with your true purpose. Focus on what you wish to manifest, and take deliberate steps toward it.

Life Lesson: Change as a Catalyst for Growth

The central life lesson in this chapter is understanding that change is essential for personal growth. Every transition, big or small, carries within it the potential for renewal. Embrace transformation as part of life's natural flow, recognizing that each ending holds the opportunity for a new beginning.

- Accept and honor change: Transformation is a fundamental part of the human experience. Rather than resisting it, honor the natural ebb and flow of life's cycles. Each transformation invites you to become a deeper, truer version of yourself.

- See endings as opportunities: Instead of fearing the end of a phase, view it as an opportunity to embrace something new. Every ending makes way for something better. Trust that the universe is guiding you toward your highest good.

- Be courageous in the face of transformation: Change can be daunting, but it also brings growth. Courageously step into the unknown, trusting that this transformation will bring you closer to who you are meant to become.

Transformation and renewal are at the very essence of life's journey. Just as the seasons change, so too do we—constantly evolving, shedding, and being reborn. By embracing these cycles of change, we cultivate fertile ground for our next great adventure. With each transformation, we become more aligned with our authentic selves, and as we let go of the old, we make room for the new.

As you journey through life, remember that change is not to be feared but celebrated. It is the ultimate source of growth, renewal, and a deeper connection to your true purpose. Embrace it fully, and let the energy of transformation propel you to new heights.

CHAPTER 15

BALANCE AND MODERATION

The Power of Balance and Patience

In a world that constantly pulls us in multiple directions, the journey toward balance and moderation requires conscious effort, patience, and self-awareness. True harmony is not found by pursuing extremes but by embracing the middle ground—where integration and patience create lasting peace. Strive for equilibrium between work and rest, action and reflection, discipline and freedom, cultivating a lifestyle where everything has its rightful place.

Balance is not about perfection or equal division but about achieving harmony between opposites. Whether it's balancing your inner world with your outer circumstances or finding peace within conflict, balance and moderation bring stability to life. The key is integration: uniting different aspects of yourself and your experiences into a cohesive whole rather than letting them work against each other.

Seeking Balance Between Extremes

Life, with all its fluctuations, often pushes us toward extremes—overwork or underachievement, indulgence or deprivation, restlessness or stagnation. While these swings can teach valuable lessons, they can also lead to burnout and discontent if not kept in check. The goal is to create a lifestyle that honors both your needs and your ambitions—a life where you can experience joy without overextending yourself or sacrificing well-being.

To seek balance between extremes:

- Recognize the pull of extremes: Acknowledge when you're leaning toward excess or deprivation. Pay attention to patterns of over-commitment or, conversely, isolation and inaction. Awareness is the first step toward achieving balance.

- Find harmony in the middle: Balance doesn't mean avoiding extremes entirely; rather, it's about centering yourself when pulled in opposing directions. Whether it's balancing work with rest, relationships with solitude, or activity with stillness, focus on moderation to create a more peaceful and grounded existence.

- Let go of perfection: Striving for perfection in any area of life often leads to imbalance. Instead of expecting flawlessness, embrace the idea of balance through compromise and flexibility. Perfection is a myth—moderation brings peace.

Cultivating Patience and Moderation

The path to balance requires cultivating patience. Life doesn't always unfold on our timetable, and pressures to rush or overexert ourselves can create stress and imbalance. Patience means trusting that everything will unfold in its own time—that healing, growth, and success happen gradually, not instantly.

To cultivate patience and moderation:

- Practice self-discipline: Finding balance sometimes requires resisting impulses that pull you away from your center. Cultivating self-discipline allows you to moderate desires and actions—not through denial but through mindful moderation.

- Learn the art of slowing down: In a fast-paced world, slowing down may feel counterintuitive, but it allows you to reconnect with your inner wisdom, observe your surroundings, and make conscious decisions. By taking things one step at a time, you avoid burnout and create space for clarity and perspective.

- Embrace mindfulness: Practices such as meditation, breathing exercises, or simply being fully present in the moment help you find balance amidst external chaos. When you cultivate mindfulness, you develop an inner state of calm and clarity, allowing you to act with wisdom and moderation.

Healing Through Integration and Balancing Opposites

Balance requires integration—not only between external and internal forces but also between different aspects of your personality and life experiences. Healing through integration means embracing the parts of yourself that may seem contradictory, such as your need for adventure and your need for security, or your desire for independence and your need for connection.

To heal through integration:

- Embrace the opposites: Life is full of dualities—light and dark, joy and sorrow, action and stillness. These are not meant to be in conflict but to complement each other. Integration doesn't mean rejecting any part of yourself; it means accepting them all and creating harmony between them.

- Balance your energy: Life can become unbalanced when you over-focus on one area and neglect others. Excessive attention to work, for example, may deplete your creativity or impact your health. Maintain balance by nurturing your physical, mental, emotional, and spiritual well-being.

- Seek harmony in relationships: Whether in personal or professional relationships, balance is key. Strive for an equal exchange of energy, respect, and understanding. Be aware of imbalances—when one person is giving too much or too little—and work toward creating a more harmonious dynamic.

Life Lesson: Striving for Balance and Harmony

Strive for balance in all areas of life. Whether balancing work with rest, action with reflection, or inner growth with outward achievement, balance is the foundation of a fulfilling and sustainable life. Integration is key—every experience, whether positive or challenging, contributes to the greater whole of who you are. By integrating these experiences, you bring harmony to your life.

To integrate lessons learned and create harmony:

- Recognize life's natural rhythms: Life moves in cycles, and balance is achieved by moving with these natural flows. Instead of resisting change, embrace the ebb and flow of your journey, knowing there will be times for action and times for rest.

- Find peace in imperfection: Striving for balance does not mean achieving perfection. Instead, it means finding peace with who you are and where you are. Be compassionate with yourself when you fall out of balance, understanding that it is part of the human experience.

- Create space for reflection: Regularly assess the balance in your life. Ask yourself: Where do I need to focus more energy? Where do I need to let go or ease up? Reflection allows you to check in with yourself and make necessary adjustments.

Conclusion: Living in Harmony with Life's Rhythms

True balance and moderation are essential for a life of peace and fulfillment. Remember that balance isn't a static destination but a dynamic, ongoing process. It requires listening to your body, mind, and soul and adjusting when necessary.

Life's journey is about integrating all experiences—the highs and lows, the challenges and joys—into a harmonious whole. By striving for balance in all aspects of life, you cultivate a sense of inner peace that will guide you through even the most turbulent times.

Balance is the foundation of a fulfilling life. Live with intention, embrace patience, and trust that by integrating all parts of yourself, you will create a life of harmony and moderation.

CHAPTER 16

OVERCOMING TEMPTATION AND LIMITATION

Breaking Free from Unhealthy Attachments and Limiting Beliefs

On every journey of personal growth, we encounter temptations and limitations—internal and external forces that attempt to hold us back. These barriers often take the form of unhealthy attachments, such as addictions to substances, material possessions, or toxic relationships. They can also manifest as self-imposed limitations—negative beliefs about our abilities or worth, fears that keep us stuck in repetitive patterns, or societal expectations that restrict our true potential.

Breaking free from these forces is a call to reclaim your power and step out of the shadows of self-doubt, fear, and dependency. To move forward on your life's path, you must confront whatever holds you back—whether it's a toxic attachment, a limiting belief, or a fear of stepping into your full potential.

Understanding Temptation and Limitation

Temptation appears in many forms—the allure of material wealth, the comfort of unhealthy habits, or the temporary relief of numbing emotional pain. Limitation, on the other hand, stems from the belief that you are not enough or that you are incapable of achieving your dreams. Both forces keep you locked in cycles of insecurity, fear, and dissatisfaction.

- Unhealthy attachments often arise from a deep sense of inadequacy or an attempt to fill an inner void. These attachments can manifest as addictions to substances, food, or unhealthy relationships that provide a false sense of security or escape.

- Limiting beliefs are rooted in past experiences or societal conditioning, creating barriers to what you believe is possible for you. These beliefs often whisper: "You are not enough." "You don't deserve happiness." "You are too old/young, too inexperienced, *or* too *flawed* to succeed."

Breaking Free from Unhealthy Attachments

The first step in overcoming temptation is awareness—recognizing the attachments that bind you. Whether it's an addiction to a substance, a pattern of seeking validation from others, or an overreliance on material possessions, breaking free requires courage and commitment.

To break free from unhealthy attachments:

- Acknowledge the attachment: Take a step back and reflect on what is holding you back. These attachments may be tangible—such as material goods or unhealthy habits—or emotional, like lingering ties to past experiences or relationships that no longer serve you.

- Understand the root cause: Unhealthy attachments often stem from deeper wounds or unmet emotional needs. Ask yourself: "What am I truly seeking from this?" Is it love, validation, comfort, or something else? Understanding the root cause allows you to address the real issue rather than just the surface-level behavior.

- Let go with intention: Breaking free requires a conscious effort to let go. Visualizing yourself releasing the attachment or creating a symbolic ritual—such as writing it down and destroying the paper—can be powerful. Understand that letting go is an act of self-love; it is about choosing your own growth over temporary comfort.

Releasing Limiting Beliefs

Limiting beliefs are especially powerful because they are often deeply ingrained in the subconscious mind. They shape the choices you make, the opportunities you pursue, and the way you see yourself in the world. Many of these beliefs are not even your own; they may have been inherited from family, culture, or society.

To release limiting beliefs:

- Identify the belief: The first step is recognizing what beliefs are holding you back. Do you believe you're not good enough to succeed? Do you feel you're too old, too young, or too inexperienced? Pinpoint the specific belief that limits your potential.

- Challenge the belief: Once identified, question it. Is *this belief* really true? Who says so? Are there *people* who have succeeded despite *facing the same obstacles?* Most limiting beliefs are based on false assumptions or outdated narratives. Disrupt these patterns by seeking evidence that proves the opposite is possible.

- Replace with affirmations: Counter limiting beliefs with positive, empowering affirmations. If your belief is "I'm not good enough," replace it with "I am worthy of success and happiness." Affirmations help reprogram your subconscious mind and open the door to new possibilities.

The Role of Fear in Limitation

Fear plays a significant role in both unhealthy attachments and limiting beliefs. Fear of failure, fear of judgment, and fear of the unknown can keep you stuck in patterns that no longer serve you. Fear-based decisions may provide short-term relief but often lead to long-term dissatisfaction.

To overcome fear:

- Face your fears: Fear grows stronger when ignored. Instead of avoiding it, confront it. Recognize that fear is often a signal of growth—stepping outside your comfort zone requires courage, but it is the only way to break free from limitation.

- Take small, courageous steps: You don't have to conquer all your fears at once. Start by taking small steps toward overcoming them. If fear is preventing you from starting a new venture, begin by taking one small action each day to bring you closer to your goal.

- Reframe failure: Fear of failure is one of the biggest limitations people face. But failure is not an endpoint—it is feedback. Reframe your perspective and see failure as an essential part of learning. Each setback is an opportunity for growth, not a reflection of inadequacy.

Life Lesson: Breaking Free from Limiting Beliefs

We are called to recognize toxic patterns and break free from self-imposed boundaries. It's about empowering yourself to move beyond fear and limitation and to choose freedom over restriction. Understand that the limitations you face are often just stories you tell yourself, stories that can be rewritten. By identifying and releasing these constraints, you make space for new possibilities, personal growth, and transformation.

Conclusion: Reclaiming Your Power

Overcoming temptation and releasing limitation is a transformative step on your journey toward self-mastery. When you break free from unhealthy attachments, limiting beliefs, and fear, you create space for your true potential to emerge. The process may not always be easy, but it is always worth it. Each step toward freedom brings empowerment, greater clarity, and a life that aligns with who you truly are.

By recognizing and dismantling the forces that hold you back, you reclaim your personal power and step onto a path of true fulfillment. Freedom comes when you release the chains—whether self-imposed or externally conditioned—and embrace the endless possibilities that await you.

CHAPTER 17

SUDDEN CHANGE AND REVELATION

Embracing Sudden Change as a Catalyst for Growth

In life, change is inevitable, but it is often the sudden and dramatic shifts that spark the most profound transformation. These moments of upheaval—when everything seems to fall apart or become chaotic—are not merely disruptions; they are powerful catalysts for renewal. Sudden change forces us to break free from outdated structures, beliefs, and patterns, creating the fertile ground necessary for personal growth and new beginnings.

Destruction, in its various forms, does not signify an end but rather the beginning of something new. It is in the crumbling of the old that we make room for the new. Sometimes, life needs to shake us awake—to dismantle the structures we've built, open our eyes to a higher truth, and force us to lct go of what no longer serves us.

The lightning bolt of revelation that accompanies these moments of dramatic change often brings clarity and realization, even if the process feels unsettling or uncomfortable at the time.

Understanding the Power of Sudden Change

When change happens suddenly, it has the unique ability to *jolt* us out of complacency and challenge the structures that may have kept us safe but stagnant. This can take many forms:

- Personal Loss or Crisis: The end of a relationship, the loss of a job, or the passing of a loved one.

- Unexpected Opportunities: A chance encounter or an unforeseen event that shifts the course of your life.

- Health Challenges: A physical or mental health crisis that forces you to re-evaluate your priorities.

- Creative Disruption: An unexpected insight or idea that challenges the way you have been thinking and working.

These events often leave us feeling disoriented, as though the world is spinning out of control. But within that chaos lies an opportunity for transformation. It is important to remember that these periods of upheaval are not *punishments* or *mistakes* but rather the universe's way of redirecting us—pushing us toward greater authenticity, growth, and clarity.

The Role of Destruction in Personal Transformation

Destruction, in this context, is not about violence or loss but rather the dissolution of old forms that no longer serve us. Just as a forest fire clears deadwood to allow new growth, the destruction of outdated structures or beliefs creates space for renewal. It is during times of intense change that we are asked to release things, beliefs, or people that have become obstacles to our growth.

- The necessity of breaking down the old: Just as a plant must shed old leaves to make space for new growth, we, too, must shed outdated identities, habits, or attachments.

- The discomfort of change: While change can bring clarity and revelation, it is important to acknowledge that it often comes with discomfort. It is normal to feel fear, confusion, or even anger when things fall apart. These emotions are a natural part of the transformation process.

- The insight gained through destruction: In the aftermath of upheaval, we often gain deeper clarity and understanding. What seemed like destruction may, in hindsight, have been an act of revelation—uncovering truths we might not have recognized before.

Life Lesson: Transformation Through Upheaval

Moments of sudden change, though unsettling, should not be feared. These are the moments when personal transformation occurs. When the familiar structures of our lives are shaken, we are given the opportunity to redefine ourselves, embrace our truth, and set a new course forward.

This chapter encourages you to:

- Trust in the process of change: Understand that upheaval is not an end but a clearing away of the old to make room for the new. These events bring with them the possibility of renewal.

- Embrace the discomfort: Though change often brings discomfort, it also leads to profound growth. Don't shy away from challenging moments—face them head-on, knowing they will lead to a greater sense of purpose and understanding.

- Look for the revelation: In every crisis or sudden change, there is a hidden truth waiting to be revealed. These moments offer the opportunity to see things clearly, understand ourselves better, and embrace a new path forward.

- Recognize the cyclical nature of change: Just as life is cyclical, so are moments of transformation. They come, they pass, and they bring new opportunities. By embracing the flow of change, you align yourself with the natural rhythm of growth and renewal.

The Path Forward After Sudden Change

Once the dust settles and the initial shock of sudden change begins to fade, the real work begins. You now have the chance to rebuild your life with new wisdom, insight, and a renewed sense of purpose. What once felt familiar may now seem limiting, and what once felt safe may now feel like a cage.

The journey forward is one of creation and rebirth. After destruction comes the task of reconstruction—but this time, with a clearer vision of who you are and what you truly want.

- Build new structures: With your newfound clarity, begin to rebuild the parts of your life that matter most, creating stronger and more authentic foundations.

- Pursue new paths: The sudden change has likely opened doors to possibilities you hadn't considered before. Follow these new opportunities with an open heart.

- Align with your true self: As old structures dissolve, you have the chance to reconnect with your authentic self, free from the limitations of outdated beliefs and fears.

Conclusion: Revelations and Renewals

We learn that moments of sudden change and revelation should not be feared or resisted. Instead, we are invited to embrace them as necessary steps in our personal transformation. These disruptive forces bring the seeds of renewal, forcing us to release what no longer serves us and make space for new growth.

Life's journey is full of unexpected twists and turns. In moments of upheaval, we are reminded that destruction is not an end but a prelude to rebirth. By trusting the process, embracing discomfort, and uncovering the revelations hidden in the chaos, we can emerge stronger, wiser, and more aligned with our true path.

As you navigate the inevitable upheavals in your life, remember that transformation is often born from the rubble. The most profound growth occurs when we step through the flames of change and emerge on the other side with a clearer sense of who we are and what we are meant to do.

CHAPTER 18

HOPE AND RENEWAL

Embrace Healing, Inspiration, and Renewed Hope

After the turbulence and challenges of life's journey, there comes a time when we must rest, heal, and restore our sense of hope. Hope and *Renewal* speaks to the profound spiritual power of hope—an energy that is always available, even during the darkest times. It's the light that gently guides us through periods of hardship, reminding us that healing is always possible and that new opportunities will eventually emerge from the shadows of our struggles.

We explore the importance of embracing spiritual renewal, inspiration, and the healing power of hope. Life often asks us to navigate through difficult periods, but these challenges are not without purpose. The road to personal transformation is rarely smooth, yet each challenge we face ultimately brings us closer to understanding our true selves and higher purpose.

The Healing Power of Hope

Hope is not just an emotion; it is an energy—a force that sustains us when everything else feels uncertain. When life has been difficult or filled with setbacks, hope can seem distant, almost impossible to grasp. Yet, hope is often quietly waiting for us to reach toward it, ready to lift us up when we need it most. It is the force that reminds us everything is temporary, and even the most challenging periods will eventually pass.

This chapter explores how hope can heal, offering a sense of peace even in the face of adversity. Hope doesn't simply mean waiting for something better to happen; it's about believing in the possibility of better. It's about having faith that life has a purpose and that our struggles ultimately contribute to the greater good of our soul's journey.

- Divine guidance: Hope often comes in the form of spiritual guidance—whether through quiet moments of reflection, messages from mentors or loved ones, or deep insights during times of stillness. Trust that this guidance will lead you toward renewal.

- Inspiration: When we embrace hope, we invite inspiration into our lives. Hope encourages us to dream again, to see possibilities where there were none before, and to reignite the passion and creativity that may have been dormant.

- Renewal: Healing begins when we allow ourselves to be open to renewal. We must shed old wounds, limiting beliefs, and fears in order to create space for the new life that is waiting for us. Hope and renewal are intertwined, as renewal is often the product of a hopeful spirit.

The Spiritual Meaning of Hope

On a deeper, spiritual level, hope reflects the trust we place in the universe or a higher power. It speaks to the belief that everything happens for a reason and that our souls are always evolving toward a higher state of being. When we experience moments of doubt, despair, or confusion, hope serves as a reminder that there is a greater plan at work—one that will ultimately guide us to our highest potential.

Hope is closely linked with faith. It encourages us to believe in the unseen, to trust that divine timing is at play, and to recognize that our current struggles are not the end of the story. In this chapter, we explore the connection between hope and the divine, learning to tap into the spiritual wellspring that supports us, even when we cannot see the way forward.

Life Lesson: Trust That Hope is Always Available

The life lesson is simple yet powerful: trust that hope is always available, and with it comes the potential for new beginnings and fresh opportunities. Even after a period of difficulty or disillusionment, hope can spark healing, bring about spiritual renewal, and guide you toward brighter days.

When life feels overwhelming, it's important to remember that hope is never lost—it may just need to be rediscovered. Hope exists as a steady companion, often hidden beneath layers of pain, fear, or uncertainty, but always present. If you open yourself to it, hope can inspire you to keep going, take one more step toward healing, and believe in the possibility of a better tomorrow.

This chapter encourages you to:

- Reignite your sense of hope: Even after setbacks or disappointments, allow hope to be your guiding star. Renew your belief in the possibility of change and growth, knowing that new opportunities will arise when you are ready.

- Trust in the flow of life: Understand that everything in life has its season. The hardest periods of our journey are often followed by times of growth and opportunity. Trust that divine timing will bring the right opportunities into your life at the right time.

- Allow yourself to heal: Healing is not a race. Be patient with yourself as you process your emotions and experiences. Hope is a gentle healer, and in time, you will see that everything you've experienced has been part of your personal growth.

- Find inspiration in the little things: Sometimes, hope comes in small doses. It might be found in a kind word from a friend, the beauty of nature, or a moment of stillness. Look for the signs of hope that are scattered throughout your daily life and let them inspire you to keep moving forward.

The Journey of Renewal

As you embrace the power of hope, renewal becomes a natural part of your life. Just as nature renews itself with each season, so too do we have the ability to renew ourselves—to shed the old and make space for the new. Renewal is a process, and it requires time, patience, and trust. It may not always come in dramatic bursts, but it appears as a steady flow of energy that brings healing, new opportunities, and the potential for growth.

We learn that the most difficult periods of our lives are often followed by moments of rejuvenation and that every cycle of life is marked by change and renewal. It is through these cycles that we become more aligned with our higher selves, discovering deeper truths and greater strength.

When you feel weary or lost, remember that hope is always within reach. In the quietest moments, hope whispers to us, offering guidance, renewal, and a path forward. Your journey of healing is ongoing, but with each step, you draw closer to a renewed sense of purpose, joy, and fulfillment.

Conclusion: Embracing the Light of Hope

We embrace hope as the force that allows us to see beyond our current struggles and limitations. Hope is not just wishful thinking; it is a spiritual truth that affirms renewal and the possibility of transformation. By trusting in hope and allowing it to guide us, we open ourselves to new beginnings, healing, and divine inspiration.

The journey may be difficult, but hope remains a steady companion, always leading us toward brighter days and deeper wisdom.

When life seems hard and the road ahead uncertain, remember that hope is always available—quietly waiting to light your path and inspire the next chapter of your journey.

CHAPTER 19

EMBRACING MYSTERY AND ILLUSION

Trust Your Intuition and Embrace the Unknown

Life is filled with mystery and illusion—moments when things seem unclear, uncertain, or confusing. In these times, we are often called to step into the unknown, trusting that the answers will reveal themselves in due time. Intuition serves as a guide, helping us navigate these moments with grace by cultivating a deep trust in our inner wisdom and embracing the spiritual mystery of life.

When faced with the unknown, it is essential to let go of the need for control and instead allow yourself to be guided by the wisdom within. At some point in our journey, we all experience moments of confusion—times when the path ahead seems clouded or when circumstances don't make sense. These moments of uncertainty are natural and, in fact, often serve as gateways to personal growth. Life's mysteries invite us to explore the world beyond our immediate understanding, teaching us to trust that the answers we seek will emerge when the time is right.

Life teaches us how to navigate confusion and illusion, both of which can obscure the truth. The key is to accept the mystery rather than resist it. It's about cultivating patience, embracing the unknown with curiosity, and having faith that all things will unfold in their own time.

Navigating Through Confusion and Illusion

We live in a world where appearances often mask deeper truths. Illusion can distort reality, while confusion makes it difficult to discern what is real from what is false. The key to navigating these forces is to develop discernment—the ability to see beyond the surface and access deeper understanding.

Illusions may take many forms: material desires, false beliefs, or the distractions of daily life. These illusions can keep us trapped in cycles of self-doubt or misunderstanding, making us question our intuition and path. However, when we embrace mystery and allow ourselves to see beyond these illusions, we open ourselves to deeper truths that can only be discovered through patience, trust, and introspection.

The practice of navigating illusion involves pausing and allowing yourself to see things from a broader perspective. It may require questioning what you think you know, stepping back from external influences, and seeking clarity from within.

The Power of Intuition

Intuition is often the guiding light in times of uncertainty. It is that subtle inner knowing that transcends logical thought and directs us toward our truest path. Your intuition does not always follow the rules of reason or logic, yet it is a powerful force nonetheless. When confusion sets in and you cannot see the full picture, your intuition will help illuminate the next step.

In this chapter, we explore how to strengthen and trust your intuition. Recognizing and honing this inner wisdom takes time, especially in a world that often prioritizes logic and rational thinking. However, intuition is a deeply personal and spiritual gift that becomes more reliable the more you trust it.

To strengthen your intuition:

- Quiet your mind: The noise of daily life can drown out your intuitive voice. Meditation, solitude, or simply taking time to be still can help you reconnect with this inner guidance.

- Listen to your body: Intuition often communicates through physical sensations—gut feelings, subtle tugs in your chest, or a sense of calm or discomfort. These physical cues can help you tune into your inner wisdom.

- Notice patterns: Intuition frequently reveals itself through patterns or recurring symbols. Paying attention to repeating signs or feelings can help you understand where to focus your energy.

- Trust what you feel: While logic has its place, there will be times when your intuition guides you in ways that don't make immediate sense. Trust it, even when the reasoning isn't clear.

Embracing the Unknown

One of the most powerful lessons in life is learning to embrace the unknown. We are often conditioned to seek certainty and control, yet the truth is that life is inherently unpredictable. Instead of fearing the unknown, this chapter invites you to step into it with openness and curiosity.

The void before creation—the space where nothing is defined—holds limitless potential. It is within the unknown that we discover new possibilities, fresh perspectives, and greater aspects of our true selves. By trusting that everything has its own timing and purpose, we can embrace the unfolding of life's mysteries without fear.

Embrace the unknown by:

- Letting go of control: Surrender to the flow of life, knowing that sometimes the best course of action is simply to allow things to unfold naturally.

- Having faith in divine timing: Trust that everything happens at the right moment, even if it doesn't make sense at the time. Believe that life is unfolding in a way that is ultimately for your highest good.

- Approaching uncertainty with curiosity: Instead of feeling anxious about the unknown, adopt the mindset of a curious explorer—excited to uncover what lies ahead.

Life Lesson: Cultivate Trust in Your Intuition

The life lesson here is about cultivating trust in your own intuition. It is a reminder that you already possess the wisdom you need to navigate life's mysteries. Everything is unfolding in its own time, and often, the key to understanding the bigger picture is to release the need for immediate answers and trust that clarity will emerge when it is meant to.

- Trust yourself: You have the inner guidance to lead you through moments of confusion. Your intuition will help you make decisions when logic alone cannot. Trust it, even when things feel unclear.

- Be patient with the process: Life doesn't always reveal itself instantly. Embrace the process of unfolding. Allow things to take their natural course, trusting that you are always exactly where you need to be.

- Embrace uncertainty: The unknown is fertile ground for growth, creativity, and self-discovery. By embracing mystery, you grant yourself the freedom to explore new possibilities and step into your fullest potential.

Conclusion: Trusting the Journey

In embracing mystery and illusion, we are reminded that life is not always meant to be understood immediately. The journey is filled with moments of confusion, illusion, and uncertainty. However, by trusting our intuition, we can navigate these times with confidence and grace.

When life feels unclear or when you are facing moments of doubt, remember that you have the wisdom within you to make decisions. The mystery of life is not something to fear—it is something to embrace. Trust that everything will unfold in its own time, and with patience and faith, you will continue to evolve and grow into the person you are meant to be.

CHAPTER 20

ENLIGHTENMENT AND JOY

Lesson: Embrace the Light of Truth, Clarity, and Joy

In life's journey, there are moments when everything feels aligned—when clarity shines through, and we experience a deep sense of joy and purpose. Enlightenment and Joy is about embracing the light of truth that illuminates our path and reveals our true selves. It encourages us to live authentically, express our true nature without fear or hesitation, and embrace the vitality that comes with living in alignment with our purpose.

Enlightenment is not a distant, unattainable goal but a living, breathing experience we can embody in each moment. It is the understanding that life is about growth, expansion, and the freedom to express our true essence. When we embrace the light of truth, we allow ourselves to radiate joy, clarity, and inner peace—spreading those energies to the world around us.

This journey invites you to step into your full potential, acknowledging your worth and the unique gifts you bring to the world. It is about recognizing the beauty and wisdom that already exist within you and using that knowledge to light the way forward. When we embrace our own brilliance, we no longer hide behind fear or self-doubt but move forward with confidence, joy, and a deep sense of purpose.

Living with Authenticity and Vitality

To live with authenticity is to align with your highest self. It means being true to who you are, shedding the masks you may have worn for protection, and embracing the parts of yourself that make you unique. True joy and fulfillment come when we express our creativity, share our gifts with the world, and align with our essence.

Living with vitality means bringing your whole self into each moment. It's about being fully present, engaging deeply in life, and celebrating all that it has to offer. When we are aligned with our true selves, life becomes a source of endless energy and inspiration. Joy is not something that happens by chance; it is a state of being that arises from living authentically.

- Self-expression: Don't hold back—let your inner light shine. Whether through your work, creativity, relationships, or how you show up in the world, allow yourself to fully express who you are. Authentic self-expression is one of the quickest paths to joy.

- Vitality: When we live authentically, we experience a profound sense of vitality. This energy comes from aligning our actions with our values and passions. It is the feeling of being fully alive, energized, and ready to engage with the world on a profound level.

- Clarity: The light of truth brings clarity. When we are aligned with our purpose, we see the world with greater understanding. Decisions become easier, and life flows more smoothly. We trust ourselves and the path ahead.

Joy as a State of Being

Joy is more than an emotion; it is a state of being. It arises naturally when we embrace our authentic selves, live with purpose, and connect to the present moment. Unlike fleeting happiness, which depends on external circumstances, joy is a steady presence that flows from within.

This chapter explores the difference between temporary happiness and sustained joy. While happiness can be momentary, joy is a deep satisfaction that comes from knowing you are on the right path and viewing life as a beautiful journey rather than a series of obstacles.

To cultivate joy in your life:

- Practice gratitude: Appreciate the beauty and blessings that surround you. Gratitude shifts your perspective, allowing you to focus on life's abundance rather than what is lacking.

- Follow your passions: Joy arises naturally when we engage in what we love. What excites you? What sparks your creativity? Follow those impulses, as they are clues to your true purpose.

- Engage in life fully: Don't hold back—immerse yourself in your experiences. Whether in relationships, work, or hobbies, joy is found in being fully present.

Living in Alignment with Your True Purpose

Living in alignment with your true purpose means making intentional choices that reflect your values and inner truth. It involves deep self-reflection and asking: Who am I? What do I stand for? How can I contribute to the world?

To live authentically is to know yourself and honor your deepest values. When you are clear about your purpose, you can align your goals, actions, and relationships to support it.

- Trust your intuition: Your intuition is a powerful compass. When you align with your inner wisdom, you are naturally led toward opportunities and experiences that bring you closer to your highest self.

- Be true to yourself: Don't conform to societal expectations or the opinions of others. Your true self is enough, and when you live from this place, you experience peace, fulfillment, and joy.

- Embrace growth: Your purpose is not a fixed destination but an evolving journey. As you grow, your purpose may shift. Trust that each phase of transformation is leading you closer to your true path.

Life Lesson: Live in Alignment with Your True Purpose

The lesson in Enlightenment and Joy is clear: Live in alignment with your true purpose. When you do, everything else in life will fall into place. You will experience a joy and fulfillment that cannot be found through external achievements or possessions. True success comes from authenticity and clarity.

To live in alignment with your purpose means:

- Releasing fear: Fear holds us back from stepping into our full potential. Let go of the fear of failure or judgment and trust in your ability to create the life you desire.

- Aligning with your values: Your values are your internal compass. When you live according to them, life feels effortless and fulfilling.

- Allowing joy to be your guide: Joy is a signal that you are on the right path. If something feels out of alignment, it is a sign to reassess and realign with your truth.

Conclusion: Embrace Enlightenment and Joy

Joy is not just a fleeting emotion but a state of being that arises when we live in harmony with our true selves. By embracing the light of truth, authenticity, and clarity, we open the door to a life full of vitality and fulfillment.

When we live in alignment with our purpose, we unlock the deepest form of success—one rooted in inner peace, clarity, and joy. Life's journey is about growth, self-expression, and the courage to be who you truly are.

The more you embrace your authenticity, the more joy and fulfillment will flow naturally into your life. Let your light shine, and live each day with the vitality and clarity that comes from living in alignment with your true self.

CHAPTER 21

AWAKENING AND TRANSFORMATION

Lesson: Awaken to Your Higher Purpose and Embrace Personal Transformation

Life is a continuous journey of growth, evolution, and awakening. This chapter explores the profound power of personal transformation and the spiritual rebirth that accompanies it. Life teaches us to awaken to our higher purpose by shedding old patterns, beliefs, and limitations that no longer serve us. Through self-reflection, introspection, and the willingness to embrace change, we can access our highest potential and align ourselves with a more fulfilling, purpose-driven life.

Transformation is often born from deep reflection and spiritual awakening. It is a process of renewal—a shedding of outdated aspects of ourselves to make way for something more aligned with our true essence.

It's about recognizing the opportunity for change within and actively choosing to evolve, learn, and grow.

Awakening requires a shift in perception—seeing life from a higher vantage point and understanding that we are not just passive participants but active creators of our experiences. It calls us to move beyond limitations, tap into inner wisdom, and trust the process of transformation. Awakening means embracing the unknown, allowing ourselves to evolve, and being open to new possibilities.

The Power of Self-Reflection

Self-reflection is a vital tool in the journey of awakening. It involves looking inward, examining our beliefs, habits, and behaviors to gain a deeper understanding of ourselves. When we take time to reflect, we can identify what no longer serves us, recognize limiting patterns, and consciously choose to release them.

- Clarity through reflection: Introspection brings clarity about our desires, goals, and the lessons life is teaching us. Reflection helps us process past experiences so they don't weigh us down, allowing us to reframe challenges as opportunities for growth.

- Breaking old patterns: Often, our past ways of thinking and behaving shape our present reality. Transformation begins when we awaken to these patterns, recognize their influence, and make the conscious choice to change. Awareness is the first step to lasting transformation.

- Emotional release: Reflection allows us to confront and release emotions that may be holding us back—anger, resentment, fear, or regret. Through self-awareness, we can make peace with our past and move forward with greater emotional freedom.

Spiritual Rebirth and Personal Transformation

Transformation and spiritual rebirth go hand in hand. To awaken spiritually means reconnecting with the essence of who we truly are—our inner light and higher self. This is a journey of rediscovery and renewal. It is an invitation to break free from societal expectations, past wounds, and outdated beliefs so we can fully embrace our potential.

- Releasing the old: Spiritual awakening requires us to let go of identities and beliefs that no longer align with our higher purpose. This includes limiting self-perceptions, toxic relationships, and habits that hinder growth.

- Embracing change: Transformation can be uncomfortable—it challenges us to step into the unknown and move beyond our comfort zones. Yet, change is necessary for growth. It allows us to develop new strengths, talents, and perspectives that align with our highest good.

- Healing and renewal: Spiritual rebirth is also a process of healing—releasing past wounds, forgiving mistakes, and making space for new beginnings. Through renewal, we cultivate confidence and compassion, empowering us to create a life that reflects our true desires.

Awakening to Your Higher Purpose

Our higher purpose is the guiding force in our lives—the deeper calling that speaks to us from within, urging us to fulfill our unique potential. Awakening to this purpose is a result of self-reflection, a willingness to change, and an openness to new experiences.

- Finding meaning: Awakening often brings a deeper sense of meaning to life. We begin to see our experiences—both good and bad—as part of a greater plan, contributing to our growth and alignment with our purpose.

- Aligning with your true self: Your higher purpose is an extension of who you truly are. Living in alignment with it means being authentic, honoring your values, and following your passions. It requires trusting yourself and making decisions that reflect your deepest truth.

- Serving a greater whole: As we awaken, we recognize that our lives are interconnected with something greater than ourselves. We begin to see how our actions contribute to the collective well-being, inspiring us to serve a greater purpose.

Embracing Transformation as a Lifelong Journey

Transformation is not a one-time event but an ongoing process. Life is cyclical, and we are always evolving. Each phase of our journey brings new opportunities for growth and awakening. We are never "finished" with our spiritual evolution; rather, we are continuously learning and expanding.

- Ongoing growth: Just as a seed continually grows into a tree, transformation is a lifelong journey. Every experience builds upon the last, helping us reach new levels of wisdom and understanding.

- The power of choice: Personal transformation is shaped by the choices we make. In every moment, we have the power to step beyond our past, choose new perspectives, and embrace the path that aligns with our highest potential.

- Trusting the process: Awakening requires faith in the unfolding journey. We may not always understand the process, but by trusting it with patience and openness, we allow it to lead us toward a life of greater fulfillment.

Life Lesson: Embrace Your Spiritual Awakening and Allow Transformation to Guide You Toward Your Highest Potential

The lesson in Awakening and Transformation is to fully embrace your spiritual awakening and trust the transformative power it brings. Life is a continuous journey of growth, and each moment offers an opportunity for renewal. As you awaken to your higher self, be willing to release what no longer serves you and step into the fullness of your potential.

Transformation requires courage, self-reflection, and a willingness to embrace change. When you allow yourself to undergo this process of renewal, you align with your highest self and open the door to a life of deeper meaning, purpose, and fulfillment.

- Awaken to your true power: Recognize the strength within you. You are more powerful than you realize, and transformation is an opportunity to step into that power fully.

- Trust the process of change: Change can be uncertain, but it is a necessary part of growth. Have faith that every shift is leading you toward something greater.

Embrace transformation as a guiding force: Rather than resisting change, welcome it as an opportunity for expansion. Each transformation is a step toward becoming the fullest expression of who you are meant to be.

Conclusion: Trust in Your Evolution

Awakening is an ongoing process—one that leads us toward greater self-awareness, deeper understanding, and a more profound connection with our true essence. As we continue to grow, we become more aligned with our purpose, more open to change, and more capable of creating a fulfilling life.

Life is a journey of becoming—of discovering who we truly are and allowing that truth to shape our path. When we embrace transformation, we step into our highest potential, trusting that each step is leading us toward a life of deeper joy, wisdom, and authenticity.

Let yourself evolve. Trust in the awakening that is unfolding within you. And know that every transformation is a sacred invitation to step into the fullness of your being.

CHAPTER 22

COMPLETION AND WHOLENESS

Lesson: Embrace the Completion of Cycles and the Achievement of Wholeness

This chapter focuses on the culmination of your journey—a moment of recognizing the wholeness you've achieved through life's cycles. It is about honoring endings, acknowledging that they naturally lead to new beginnings, and understanding that every phase of your journey is an essential part of the greater whole.

Life is a continuous cycle of learning, growing, and evolving. Every experience, whether joyful or challenging, adds to the rich tapestry of who you are becoming. Completion is not merely the end of a chapter; it is the recognition that you have integrated the lessons, wisdom, and growth from that phase. It is the moment when you stand in your wholeness, having gathered the insights and strength needed to step into the next stage of your life.

Completion signifies fulfillment. It represents the sense of wholeness that comes from embracing both the triumphs and the trials, knowing that they have led you to a place of inner harmony and understanding. This chapter encourages you to step back and reflect on all you've accomplished, recognizing that the conclusion of one cycle simply marks the beginning of another.

The Power of Integrating Life's Experiences

Completion is about more than finishing a task or achieving a goal— it is about integration. Life unfolds in phases, each one imparting new lessons. Taking time to reflect on these experiences ensures that we fully absorb their wisdom. Without integration, we risk carrying unresolved emotions or unfinished lessons into the next chapter, preventing us from moving forward with clarity.

- Honoring the Journey: Completion invites you to honor your journey, both the easy and difficult moments. Every experience, no matter how challenging, has contributed to your growth. You have gained lessons that are now embedded in your being. Pause and reflect on how far you've come, and take a moment to celebrate your progress.

- Embracing Wisdom: As you reach the completion of a phase, you begin to recognize the wisdom that has emerged from your experiences. You may see how your choices, mistakes, and victories have all woven together into a deeper understanding of yourself and the world around you. This wisdom does not come solely from successes—often, the greatest lessons arise from struggles, as they teach us resilience, adaptability, and transformation.

- Integrating the Past and Present: Completion allows you to integrate the past with your present self. Rather than viewing past experiences as separate from you, you begin to see them as vital pieces of your journey. By embracing your history, you acknowledge how it has shaped who you are today. This integration brings you closer to your true self—the person you were always meant to become.

The End of One Chapter, The Beginning of Another

While completion invites reflection on all you have learned and achieved, it also signals the beginning of the next cycle. Life does not stand still. Every phase of completion opens the door to new growth and exploration. Wholeness is not a static state; it is a dynamic, evolving process, continually deepening as we expand our awareness and understanding.

- Cycles of Growth: Every completed cycle leads to new opportunities for learning. The conclusion of one life chapter marks the start of another. Even after reaching a sense of wholeness, there will always be new challenges, new lessons, and new experiences to explore. Each cycle builds upon the last, laying the foundation for deeper levels of wisdom, self-discovery, and fulfillment.

- Renewed Possibilities: With completion comes the emergence of fresh possibilities. When we take time to reflect on and integrate the lessons of the past, we step into the future with greater clarity and intention. The next chapter is not about starting over from nothing—it is about building upon all that has come before, using past experiences to create a richer, more meaningful future.

- Continuing the Journey: Completion is not an ending—it is a renewal. It signals your readiness to embark on a new journey, equipped with the wisdom and experience gained from the past. Embrace this new beginning with an open heart, knowing that each phase of life serves as a stepping stone toward greater understanding, personal evolution, and alignment with your highest potential.

Life Lesson: Celebrate Your Journey, Integrate Your Experiences, and Embrace the Wisdom Gained Through Every Phase of Life

The lesson in Completion and Wholeness is to honor your journey, embracing the wisdom that emerges from every phase of life. Completion is a natural and essential part of the cycle of growth, and taking the time to reflect on each stage allows for deeper appreciation and integration.

- Celebrate Your Achievements: Acknowledge and celebrate all you have accomplished. Whether big or small, every milestone in your journey is significant. Recognize your growth, resilience, and courage. Every victory, no matter how seemingly minor, has contributed to your wholeness.

- Embrace the Wisdom of Each Phase: Every stage of life holds unique lessons. When you look back, see not only the challenges but also the transformation they inspired. Recognize that each phase has propelled you toward greater self-awareness and personal growth.

- Live in Wholeness: Wholeness is not about perfection—it is about integration. It means honoring all aspects of yourself, including your successes and your struggles. Wholeness is a state of embracing the totality of your experiences, recognizing how they have shaped you, and understanding that growth is a continuous, ever-unfolding journey.

Conclusion: The Ever-Expanding Journey of Wholeness

Completion and Wholeness teaches us that life unfolds in cycles, each one bringing us closer to our full potential. By celebrating our journey, embracing the wisdom gained from each phase, and integrating past experiences, we create a strong foundation for continued growth.

Wholeness is not a final destination—it is a continuous process of becoming. It is an ever-deepening relationship with yourself, one that evolves as you embrace each chapter of life with openness and trust. With every completed cycle, you step further into the fullness of who you are meant to be.

So, as you honor the past, celebrate the present, and step into the future, know that each ending is merely a doorway to new beginnings. Life is an ongoing journey of transformation, and every phase is an essential part of your unfolding story.

Embrace your wholeness. Trust the cycles of life. And step forward with the knowledge that every chapter—past, present, and future—is bringing you closer to the deepest expression of your true self.